Footprints
on
Monte Cassino

Jerry Kubica

Produced on "CreateSpace Independent Publishing Platform"

Editing by Pamela Brown MA
Cover design by Pamela Brown
All rights reserved.

ISBN-13: 978-1495201974

ISBN-10: 149520197X

DEDICATION

For my grandsons Stephen and Thomas.

Perhaps before the battles for Monte Cassino will have passed into textbook history, they too will want to follow the footprints of their great-grandfather Józef Kubica. Hopefully, this story will encourage them to do so.

A note from the Author

I was born in 1939 in what was then Poland, and is now Belarus. I grew up a happy boy in India, oblivious of the

carnage of WW2, and came to the UK in 1947 for the family to be reunited with my father serving in General Anders' Polish 2nd Corps.

Only very much later in my life I learned of the horrors of our family's deportation to Siberia in April 1940, the death of my little sister in Tehran on the way to our freedom, my father's years in Stalin's GULAG camps, our saviour – the Anders Army – and the battle for Monte Cassino, and the bitterness and grief of the Polish people at the loss of their homeland to the Communist regime. Poland for our family was closed; we could only expect prison for my father and persecution for the rest. So I grew up and grew old in the UK; I have lived and worked in the USA and in France for a number of years yet, each time, I returned to the UK – this was my homeland, the only home I knew.

In a much belated recognition of my parents' struggle and sacrifice I set out on a journey to feel the history of those years, and to pass it on to my children and grandchildren. Over the past ten years I have travelled with a backpack in Western Europe, Belarus, Ukraine, Uzbekistan and searched for the footprints of the GULAG across Russia and Kazakhstan.

This book, *"Footprints On Monte Cassino"* reflects the scenarios conjured in my mind of the mental anguish, inhumanity, and the glory on the battlefield as I walked the trails left by the men who took part in this bloody battle. It is the first of my stories on the theme *"In The Footsteps Of Our Fathers"* to be published in support of the Charity, "Our Roots Trust" of which I am a founder member.

January 2014

CONTENTS

Preface and Acknowledgments

My father served in the General Anders Army, Polish 2nd Corps, 5th *Kresowa* Infantry Division, and took part in the battle for Monte Cassino. He didn't come out of it unscathed, but he came out whole and alive. He didn't talk much about it, or perhaps I was too preoccupied with my own life to hear. Unfortunately, he died at the age of 66 - much too soon for me to put my arm around his shoulders, and ask and listen; and Monte Cassino lay dormant in my heart and mind until now.

At the age of 73, I accepted the challenge to walk the trails on the battlefield of Monte Cassino – I did it to raise funds for *Our Roots Trust* charity, and I felt I owed it to my father.

At the end of April 2012 the Italian spring was beginning to turn into an early summer, the sun was strong but the heat still quite bearable. I did the "Polish tourist trails" and, after five days, went home quite pleased that, somehow, I coped. But to my surprise, Monte Cassino had grabbed my heart and mind; and the moment I arrived back home I knew I had to go back – urgently.

So I set out for the second time in the last few days of June. Now, the sun was absolutely cruel, temperature in the upper thirties, heat - unbearable. But there was no turning back – I had to walk all the paths our fathers had walked in those memorable days of May 1944, and to do it alone lost in deathly silence and in the beautiful but sometimes cruel Nature. I had to sweat the Monte Cassino "bug" out of my heart and mind. But after five days on the Massive, I suddenly realised I was nearing utter heat exhaustion and collapse; I had no other choice but to take the next plane home. And still the "bug' held, it would not relent, my obligation was not yet met.

So I set out for the third time, in late October, and this time, Nature was good to me, welcoming… 25th October was an absolutely perfect day for walking the Inferno Trail. The next and following days the air was thick with wetness, washed down with short, sharp showers, but how perfect for experiencing the ruins of San Pietro, walking the Big Bowl, and dipping into the "void".

For me, Monte Cassino turned out to be a unique and unforgettable experience, for even now it haunts me and draws me to it; and I know I will have to return one day to plumb the depth of the Big Bowl, to pay my homage to the "Lord of Cassino" and to follow the footprints left by the Irish and the French…

I have personally experienced none of what men have suffered in battle, but what I have read and heard, and seen on this journey has left an indelible impression on me; it followed me with every step. My story reflects the scenarios conjured in my mind of the mental anguish and the inhumanity and glory on the battlefield as I followed the footprints of our men fighting this bloody battle; naturally, the contribution of the 2nd Polish Corps led by General Anders is perhaps closest to my heart, but men from other nations fought equally bravely and gave their lives for the freedom of others – the Americans, men from Britain and its Commonwealth and Empire, the French and men from its Colonies, even men from as far away as Brazil… so many.

I will be happy to share this experience with you. The 20 photographs in the book give testimony to what Man can do to Man. The material I have read is listed in the bibliography. Some sources shook me to the core, and I would like to express here my appreciation for their contribution to my experience and my story. In particular:

Melchior Wańkowicz – for his powerful hot-off-the-battlefield reporting presented in his book 'Bitwa o Monte Cassino', General Władysław Anders – the commander of the 2nd Polish Corps - for the Polish saga encapsulated in his book 'Bez Ostatniego Rozdziału', Młotek Mieczysław (Editor) – for an exhaustive history of the 3rd DSK of the 2nd Polish Corps in "Historia Trzeciej Dywizji Strzelców Karpackich", Matthew Parker – for an exhaustive and fascinating presentation of the battles around the Monte Cassino massive in his book 'Monte Cassino', for the New Zealand Ministry of Culture and Heritage, and for the Alexander Turnbull Library at National Library of New Zealand - for their kind permission to reproduce the images of photographs from The Official History of New Zealand in the Second World War 1939-1945 collection.

I would also like to express my thanks to Pamela Brown for the encouragement and support she gave me in the writing of my story, and my appreciation of her editorial comments and suggestions.

1

And the bell tolls

A horizontal line of intense lights high up in the sky, seemingly detached from this world, was focusing on me. One, two, three... ten; the eleventh too was searching for me from around the corner. The half-moon this night, its profile still sharp against the sky, left my view submerged in blackness; even the spy satellite at its tail didn't help to unravel the enigma. These lights... were they angry, resentful of my presence? Were they not perhaps saying: how can you, old man, finally come here for the first time sixty-eight years to the day after the event; how dare you look up at us from the comfort of a soft bed in a 3-star hotel? Is this what your father had fought for; is this what his 1,051 Polish colleagues had given up their lives for on these hills? No, of course not. I know - they went...

jak zawsze "Za Waszą i Naszą Wolność" się bić
[as always to fight for Your and Our Freedom]

The lights throbbed persistently; ants began to creep up my spine and numb my brain. I must have eventually yielded to their hypnotic effect; was I dreaming, or re-living something from the past, some memories, or stories I have heard perhaps...

- Mom... I am scared... I don't want to go there...
- Come on son, hold my hand... we've come a long way to get here. We have to go. Maybe we

will find them... We don't have a whole day, you know; let's take a short cut - straight up.

- Mom... look at these huge holes in the ground? And look... trees have no branches or leaves, they are all black... and look... What's that mom? A cave?

- No, no... that was a German bunker; and those small rectangular holes you see in the rock-face... German sharpshooters from behind them were picking off Polish soldiers. Watch out, mind where you step, and don't kick anything.

- Mom... look, look... there in that hole... ugh! What's that? Oh, look Mom... books and papers on the ground by that backpack...

- Ah yes... let me see... what's this book... Good Lord! Look where it opens...

Thou shall not Kill...
Love thy neighbour as thyself...
Thou shall have no other Gods...

- It's the Bible; it's in Polish! I wouldn't have thought Polish soldiers had space for a Bible in their backpack... the Ten Commandments! But the letters are so small I can't see how anyone would have been able to take notice of them. No wonder we have wars. And look here:

Turn the other cheek...
Put your sword away...

Other pages are soaked in blood. Oh my! Look at the first page! *"Za Waszą Wolność i Naszą"* and someone has written - KILL - in huge letters! No problem reading this message… that's what every soldier saw first; that's what this whole thing was about; that's what your dad and uncles came here to do… KILL!

- Mom, look, a photograph fell out of the book… what is it?
- Let me see… Oh, it looks like the Holy Mass is being held in the open… before the battle, perhaps… and the priest - no it's a bishop - is blessing the troops… giving them absolution for all the killing?
- What's "*absolution*" Mom?
- The guarantee by the bishop that God will forgive your dad for killing Germans.
- What about German soldiers… will they go to hell for killing Polish soldiers?
- Son… I don't know any longer.
- Mom, what is "*Za Waszą Wol…*" in English?
- That means "For Your Freedom and Ours" Ah, these Poles! Why can't they go to war like the Brits - fight for something clear and simple, like: "For the King and Country" or like the Americans, with their hand on their heart - for "America". Why must the Poles always fight for some ridiculous ideals like: "*Za Waszą Wolność i Naszą*" or "*Bóg, Honor, Ojczyzna*". Oh, that's "God, Honour and Homeland" in English. If only they had fought for just "*Ojczyzna*", for their Homeland - then they might have saved it from catastrophe!

- Oh Mom, look… a bayonet! Can I take it?
- Don't be silly, of course not; it must have been overlooked by the clearers.

- Mom… can I take that… look, it has a Polish eagle still on it… can I?
- Well, we can't leave a Polish soldier's cap lying around. Let's take it home; just get the soil off it; it will be a memento dear to our hearts.

- Come on son; we have some way still to go; it's a long way to the Monastery.
- Mom… look, there's some writing on that ruined wall… *"ręka, noga…"* What does it say Mom?
- Oh… *"ręka, noga, mózg na ścianie."* I don't believe it!
- What is it in English, Mom?
- "arm, leg, brain spattered on the wall". You know, that's what boys used to say amongst themselves when they were talking about Germans… when they were too young to join the army. It was a kind of an oath of solidarity… that's what they were going to do to the Germans when they finally got their chance. Some of these boys had to grow up very, very quickly, and they never forgot their youthful oath.

- Mom! I am going to be sick! Look what's there! Horrible… is it a dead body?
- Don't look. Turn your head away. Yes… that's what's left of a soldier… can't tell whether it's a Polish or German soldier… they should have cleared all dead soldiers by now. Come on…

- Mom… you said my little sister was dead… died in Teheran… was she like the soldier there too?
- Son, don't mention Teheran! I can't stop my tears when I hear Teheran"…and at the same time I want to swear at our Allies!

- Why Mom… why Teheran, Mom?

- Oh, son! Two tragedies in Teheran… Your little sister died there from meningitis; she was so good to you, always looked after you. No, no, she was never like that soldier there! She was beautiful, and she went straight up to heaven. That's our own, personal tragedy we will never forget. But there was also a second tragedy in Teheran; it hit all the Poles - your father and all Polish soldiers fighting here alongside the British, dying here for the Allied cause, dying for that crazy idea – *"Za Waszą Wolność"*. The same Allies, our friends, gave half of Poland away to Stalin in exchange for some future land that belongs to Germany! They gave away your Homeland and your home to the bloody Communists, to Stalin! They were naïve… that's political expediency for you; that's what it was! No friendship, no loyalty, no duty on their part - except from our side!

- Come on son, time to start going back home.

- Home? Where's home Mom?

- Why, it's in London now. I told you we can't go back to Poland, not after what's happened in Teheran.

- But you said our home was in Scotland Mom?

- No longer son. You are too young to remember… but in 1941, when Polish soldiers came over from France to Scotland, Scottish people were very happy to see them. Polish soldiers were stationed there to protect Scottish borders; they helped local people on their farms, helped with other work… Scottish girls married Polish soldiers… everybody was happy. But when

Hitler attacked Russia in 1941, Stalin became a great "friend" of Britain and America, and joined them in the fight against Germany. But even before the German attack on Russia, Stalin had already grabbed our Homeland and launched a propaganda war against the Poles... and Mr Churchill, and the Scottish people listened and believed him.

- What's "*propaganda*" Mom?
- Lies! You see, Mr Churchill was happy to have the Polish Corps under General Anders alongside the British forces fighting the Germans in Italy. Then, as Russia grew stronger militarily with American aid, Stalin became a much more important friend than the Poles... and Churchill saw the Poles as a bloody nuisance because they hated Stalin and kept on reminding Churchill why he went to war, and demanded their country back! And Scottish people listened to Stalin's propaganda in Great Britain, and began turning against the Poles, even beating them up in the streets of Glasgow. And when the war ended, Scottish soldiers were returning home from the front. They all wanted jobs... so trade unions didn't want the Poles anymore; go back home you bloody foreigners they shouted... And even after the battle of Monte Cassino... and not only in Scotland. No, it wasn't very nice of them...

But I was not at home this night; I was comfortably in bed in a hotel in Cassino. Suddenly, hair rose on my scalp – the barrels of the ten machineguns seemed to look straight into my eyes; one just around the corner covered their flank. There was absolutely nothing to obstruct their line of fire; they didn't even bother to cut the lights so cock-sure were they of their invincibility! One move by me in my bed, one soft touch on the trigger by them, and they would have blown my brains out; indeed, there would be nothing left of me but my "arm, leg and brain spattered on the wall". They could blow me out of bed and turn the hotel into smithereens; nay, the entire town of Cassino, and even the terrain way beyond the Rapido River was at their mercy. Who in their right mind would dare assault the town of Cassino in this situation? Yet the Allies did – were they lacking intelligence, or just military intelligence?

From somewhere deep in the night, the sound of a church bell began to stir my consciousness – pure but sombre, muffled by distance and night air. Again and again, and again… it struck regularly, only every now and again it reverberated, just a little, as if the ringer erred inadvertently. Subconsciously, I started counting… five, six… ten… fifty! one-hundred! one hundred-and-fifty… and still it continued! Unbelievable! What message was it sending my way? Was it tolling just for me, or for the 1,051 men resting in the Polish War Cemetery? Was it perhaps reminding the world in all its time zones that here

ZA WASZĄ WOLNOŚĆ I NASZĄ
MY ŻOŁNIERZE POLSCY
ODDALIŚMY
BOGU - DUCHA
ZIEMI WŁOSKIEJ – CIAŁO
A SERCA – POLSCE

[For your freedom and ours / We Polish soldiers / Gave / God – our soul / Italian soil – our bodies / Our hearts – to Poland]

...151, 152... 175... 191! Perhaps the toll continued through the night, painfully recounting to 1,051, but when I opened my eyes, daylight was streaming into my hotel room through the open balcony door; the air was calm, fresh, invigorating.

2

Yet they did; they went…

A wall of green hid the world from my view in flamboyant young woods and shrubs covered in delicate leaves of spring. At a distance of only few yards from my balcony, the wall receded steeply up and up, and up to the peak of Monte Cassino crowned by the Benedictine Monastery. For a brief minute or two, perhaps for my benefit only, the light from the halos of a hundred, perhaps a thousand angels bathed the Monastery in brilliant, scintillating, golden sunlight, encircling it, protecting it from… Mankind; never again would they allow the repeat of that infamous day of 15th February 1944 when the Monastery was bombed into a pile of rubble. Never again, never again… never?

That glorious view faded, and I was left dumbfounded… surely they couldn't, surely it would have been suicidal for troops to assault the Monastery from the town of Cassino lying at its feet… yet they did! Up an incline of 45° or more, up layered terraces ten feet high, through terrain pitted with bomb craters, exhausted and weighed down by the arms and ammunition they had to carry, sweat blinding their eyes… and then only to face German machinegun nests, snipers, mortar, artillery fire… surely! They were mad! Yet they went… The flamboyant young woods, those delicate leaves of spring that cheered my soul and brought a smile to my face suddenly disappeared - only the greyness, the opaqueness of smoke screen and fog, the acrid smell of explosives, and pain, anguish and wrath remained; and the bodies of the human dead, dead mules, and the wounded and dying strewn on the blood-soaked ground among decapitated trees replaced that glorious view. Surely... they must have been mad! Yet they did; they went...

But if our men went up these slopes burdened by arms and ammunition and facing death – surely, the least I can do is follow their footprints, their bloody paths to glory or death. Only my age burdens me, but even this I can alleviate with vitamins and a pocket-full of pain killers. Surely... they faced German mines, machineguns, mortars, artillery... all I will face today is the wrath of vipers in their love-making season, ticks, loose rock, overgrown and forgotten paths, vertigo... All how insignificant in the context of their sacrifice.

Rocca Janula – Castle Hill

And that castle on the hill that I can see from my hotel window? My telephoto lens brings into sharp focus the rock upon rock, upon un-scalable rock on which it sits. For some reason, that thousand halos had not embraced it. It just sat there, enigmatic, its ruined keep protruding above tree tops, its walls solid, grey, one entrance into its bowels, no other openings to let any light in or let any life out. It looks small, inconsequential in its setting - a toy castle in the 21st Century you may think - yet a foreboding guardian of access routes to the Monastery from Cassino town; its enigma, its magnetism is irresistible - I have to go.

Just a few hundred yards from my hotel, just past the first hairpin turn in the road to the Monastery, the German bunker at the foot of the hill will stop you from walking past. You can't ignore it, not even now - it's looking into your hotel window, staring you in the face. The bunker is shattered now but part of its wall facing the town still stands; four apertures, each 9x9 inches square are clearly visible even though tufts of grass and soil block them now, but back then... German sharpshooters watched you from behind them - stick your head out, and you wouldn't even hear the "ping" nor see the small round hole in your head. A little to the right, wedged into the hairpin elevation a small shrine, now vandalised, brings into sharp focus the contradiction between Man's professed beliefs and his deeds; a border of yellowish grass runs along its base, and amongst its wisps – red poppies...

Clamber over the embankment by the shrine, a narrow crumbly path leads up the hill - what a strange environment! Shadowy darkness permeates the vegetation... ruins of old stone walls, arches, columns... was it an old castle, a church perhaps... dead and forgotten history? Follow the path... and you enter the world of the living: clothes strewn on the ground, heaps of rubbish, mattresses... today's living-quarters amongst what's left of an age-old church or residence and... silence. No one answers to my repeated calls of "buon giorno!" Look up, look around you... ruins here, there... a steep climb into the unknown, into those rocks upon rocks, into those foreboding heights... and the castle somewhere, up there. That's the way New Zealand troops had taken to take the castle... and paid with blood. No, not for me... not today.

I will take the castle by an easier, safer route. Past the first hairpin turn in the road to the Monastery a small shrine catches my eye – now empty, devastated... and almost next to it masses of rubbish piled high by the living of today. A little further, a massive shelter or bunker sits hidden in the vegetation; the steel girder that once supported its roof now rests with one end on the ground, wild growth bars the entrance; a well trodden path meanders in the growth down to the dump I had come upon earlier. Further along the road, another massive German defence installation, its solid roof level with the edge of the road, now partly converted for occupation... by the living of today.

Half-hour, one hour... another hairpin turn, and I am level with the castle. Metal fencing with padlocked gate is the first obstacle... clamber over it, and the last fifty yards separate me from the looming wall of the castle. No guns or ammunition, no dead left on this battlefield now, nor any living men or guard dogs today, only building materials and a digger – a sure sign reconstruction of the castle is underway; is it with history in mind, or is it to be yet another residence for the rich and powerful?

A modest memorial on the way stops you immediately rushing the walls:-

THE ESSEX REGIMENT
TO COMMEMORATE THE GALLANTRY
AND SACRIFICE OF ALL RANKS OF

THE 1/4th BATTALION
THE ESSEX REGIMENT
WHO FOUGHT IN THE BATTLE OF
CASSINO 1944
AND IN THE MEMORY OF ALL MEMEBERS
OF THE REGIMENT WHO GAVE
THEIR LIVES IN ITALY

Such a small castle, only some 34x40m., yet it had taken so many lives. All the blood spilt within and around its thick walls had long ago percolated into its rocky base, all the dead and injured cleared, all scrap, explosives, and materiel removed, only the keep shows signs of the raging battle… its innards collapsed into a pile of rubble but it still rises proudly and defiantly well above the rebuilt walls; a horizontal steel girder sticks out of it as if to show that it's ready for more victims to dangle from its end.

But from close up, the castle loses its enigma - the gateway over which such intense fighting took place has been rebuilt, two of its walls are now as new, foundations for structures within its walls laid. But scramble over the piles of rubble and through a breach in the wall… look east - a magnificent view of Cassino… and what a magnificent position from which to kill anyone, or destroy anything in the town at its feet; look down – a chasm… and gingerly you back away into the safety of its walls! Who, in their right mind, could have hoped to take the hill and the castle! Yet the New Zealanders did; they scaled the near vertical wall of the ravine, stormed the gateway, took prisoners, and dug in. Men from the Essex Regiment came to relieve them, but by then the

Germans had realized how absolutely important the castle was in controlling the town of Cassino and any movement of Allied troops up towards Hangman's Hill and the Monastery, so they launched counter attack after counter attack against the defenders in the castle... a blood bath resulted, but the men from Essex held on.

Cassino Town

The town of Cassino bathes in sunlight today, warm, fresh air, quiet, relaxed. People, both young and older, promenade along Corso de la Republica, or sit outside cafes sipping aperitifs, snacking on pizzas; you have to search the streets to find a supermarket. I could happily come here on vacation... it's just that when I look west, towards those enticing green hills, the Monastery, way up there on the summit, generates a feeling of perpetual unease. It sits there like a medieval castle in splendid isolation neither lording over the town nor protecting it, but overlooking my every move, my every thought.

Who now remembers the Monastery's day of doom - February 15th 1944? The day the silver devils of US Strategic Air Force unleashed their wrath; bombs rained on the Monastery, and continued to fall as wave after wave, after wave of Flying Fortresses flew over it. Its ten-foot thick walls crumbled, its 1,400-year history crumbled... what life could have survived inside? The entire world feared this will have to happen... argued against the bombing, prayed it will not come about... but in the name of military necessity, in the name of saving even one Allied life, it did happen. The world stopped and, in shock and awe, witnessed something unimaginable; and the Commanders of Allied forces on the Cassino front stood on distant hills opposite the Monastery overcome with the unforgettable "beauty" of the spectacle they themselves had unleashed!

But how could anyone have been surprised, or shocked by the event. Those eleven lights in the darkness of the night boring into my eyes, those eleven machinegun barrels aimed at my head . . . how could anyone expect any soldier to assault German emplacements on Monte Cassino when those massive walls were perceived to be full of enemy; surely, it would have been sure death – from a bullet or fear! Who at the time could have categorically assured New Zealand troops that Germans were not waiting for them inside the Monastery? No, the Monastery had to be destroyed. But the Monastery didn't die. Ten years later it rose like the Phoenix; it was rebuilt, and people now come from far to see it in its glory, to marvel at the magnificent views from its walls, and to look upon the town of Cassino at their feet, as I look at it today.

And who in the town of Cassino now remembers the "Ides of March" of 1944; who still remembers Cassino's own day of doom? At 08.15 on 15th March, the earth trembled as the first wave of silver devils, in perfect formation, flew over the town. In wave after wave they flew dropping 1000-pound bombs until the job was done, until the town of Cassino was wiped out! It was a fine morning – like today – when the bombing started, but as it progressed, the entire town and the world around it became enveloped in an impenetrable cloud of dust and smoke. The silver devils didn't have the Garmin GPS I hold in my hand today - they strayed from their target, and Allied bombs fell on Allied troops on the hillside nearby, and on civilian population as far as Venafro twenty five kilometres away! And when they left, there was no longer Corso de la Republica, or Via Casilina, no railway station or any other structure left intact - only huge craters, rubble, and the dead, wounded and those still alive buried under it.

General Freyberg, Commander of the elite New Zealand Corps covered in glory from the fighting in North Africa, sent his best fighting men to take the rubble but, to their great surprise, not all in the rubble were dead! German paratroopers survived, if only two or three hundred… but they were Hitler's elite. For them, every mound of rubble, every building destroyed, every basement, every gap in a wall was now an Allied-sent cover for sniping, for machine-gunning, for hand-to-hand fighting… For them it was an honour to die for Herr Hitler; and their orders were to hold the town at all cost. It was no use sending Allied tanks in – there were no streets or other ways left for them to follow, or buildings, or barricades for tanks to knock down… so the German paratroopers held the New Zealanders at bay. And the next day the rains came - it poured… it filled the bomb craters with water and turned the rubble and dust into quagmire. And the Allied tanks got stuck, and the New Zealanders got stuck… and then came German paratroopers' counter attack, and then German reinforcements began to infiltrate from Monte Cassino…

No... the rubble couldn't be taken, not so easily, not so quickly, not from German elite troops. And they had learnt a few tricks from Montgomery at El Alamain. Just a hundred yards from my hotel stands Hotel Continental. It looks as insignificant today as the rubble it was then, but well hidden in that rubble sat a big German tank... only its turret and gun protruded, and it showered death on any man or tank that appeared in its sights. No one dared come out into the open in daylight; only perpetual smoke screens added some measure of protection for the men from New Zealand. Curiously, the receptionist at today's Hotel Continental assures me that this is not the Hotel Continental of 1944 - that one no longer exists - but step out into the street and there, facing you stands... the tank, its cannon ready, even today, as then, to blast you out of this world.

This was not the first attempt to take the town Cassino. Following on from the bombing of the Monastery, General Kippenberger, in command of the 2nd New Zealand Division sent his Maori troops to take the railway station. In these wet and wintry conditions, the valley of the Rapido River was flooded and the station was standing in what was virtually a flooded plain. The only possible access to the station buildings for men and tanks was along the railway causeway, but this, just as it is today, was in full view of the spying eyes on the Cassino mountain. Leading Maori companies went in - big, strong, fighting men... and they nearly succeeded... but then German counter attacks came, and then German tanks came... but no reinforcements for the Maoris came... and the brave Maori fighters, ready to die – all for one, one for all - were nearly all wiped out.

Today, the rubble has gone, memories have faded… it's a nice, almost parochial railway station with helpful service personnel; trains will now take you on to Rome any time, any day in just a couple of hours… no more blood, no deaths - it's fun time, it's tourist time. The river Gari, perhaps ten feet wide at the approach to the station, ripples fast and happily within its banks, its water, fresh and cool, leaves condensation on the surface of my plastic water bottle, its world reposes in lush greenery enveloped in silence; a kayaker riding its rapids suddenly flashes by; and, suddenly… Booom! The sound jerked me upright! Artillery exploded into action, anti-aircraft guns opened up, machineguns barked from somewhere in the mountains east of town! It's as if Cassino was trying to fill-in the picture for me - how it was then, how it sounded back in May 1944 for, five or ten minutes later, the firing exercise and the audio show were over - all was back to normal; life goes on. But just imagine - 1600 and more artillery guns firing their salvos all at the same time! 1600 guns at the same time! 1,600!

The Monastery

Looking up from the railway station, you just might catch the top of a vehicle floating easily up or down the thin line of serpentine leading up to the Monastery on Monte Cassino. It's so easy today, take a minibus or walk the nine kilometres if you can – nothing will be in your way; but back in April 1944, every turn in the serpentine, every terrace, every hillock bristled with German bunkers and machineguns supported by mortars and artillery on still higher ground.

…so I trudge up the mountain - backpack, walking poles, bottle of mineral water… Up and up and up… temperature in upper 30's… 38'C! Sweat, stamina, all my reason is draining out of me… my self-preservation instinct wants to put a stop to it… heat exhaustion… heat exhaustion… heat… give it up boy, give it up! But how can I stop, give up… the history of this place is riveting, it's all around me. One hour, two… more and more laboriously up and up… The sun is cruel today, it casts no shadows; the road surface and the rocks reflect its light and radiate the heat back straight into my face, sparse grass withers in the heat…

A tree – mercifully, a tree! Ah… rest, rest! Amazingly, a lone tree just inside the hairpin is flourishing in this burning sun; the shadow from its broad crown protects its roots, and like the Good Samaritan, it comforts me too. A car or two, a moped, come down the hairpin bend fast almost running over my feet, and veer away in surprise and amazement at seeing me, but they should have seen my blood-red, sweat-drenched shirt spread out on the rocks to dry… and I too look around in amazement!

Facing me across the road, a small shrine built into a rock, a plaque on the stone beside it… or was it not a well-camouflaged entrance to a German bunker? And a little to the left… the Hangman's Hill – a hump of bare rock, a huge heat-blister on the back of Monte

Cassino, the hunchback of Notre Dame guarding the Monastery! It's hard to imagine how anyone could have survived exposure on this hump - not only to the sun, but to the machine guns on the Monastery Hill... yet the Ghurkhas did! They took this hump in savage fighting in February 1944, they were only three hundred yards from the Monastery then, but it was easier to take the hump than to hold it - no reinforcements could get through to them, no food, no water, ammunition running out... they cowered on the hump for eight days, suffered heavy losses and, finally, had to abandon their positions. All the blood has been washed off by rain now, munitions and mines cleared... can't I scale it then? I put my foot onto it... one step, two, three... no, no, not today; I will come again, when I am younger, stronger, like the Ghurkhas... perhaps then.

Laboriously up and up along the serpentine... two hours, three! It's becoming easier and easier to find an excuse to stop, let the head rest a little on the chest, lean heavily on my walking poles... look at the Castle far below my perch... admire the views of Cassino and the mountains in the far distance... ah, here's what's left of a German bunker... and there's yet another... and here's a section of the 1944 track that went up the hill – steep, narrow, overgrown - it was good enough for legwork and mules, but not for today's traffic... and wasn't that a snake rustling in the grass... and those rocky slopes in between the terraces, fenced in... are they perhaps still not cleared of mines or unexploded ammunition? Hairpin-1... 2... the seventh... and suddenly, a great surprise and absolute relief overcomes me, I am at the foot of the

Monastery! I did it, I did it… just! And thank you St Benedictine for that infinite supply of drinking water from that outdoor spout, and for that car-park bollard I can sit on by the entrance to the Monastery!

I didn't drink much water the first day in this blistering sun - I didn't want to or didn't need to drink, so I thought, but in the night, my thigh muscles ached, cramp seized my calf muscles… a painful and most unusual experience for me. Perhaps "old folk's tales" are true – you must drink, always drink… your muscles need water. Perhaps I will now stop smiling condescendingly at joggers, young and old, carrying water bladders on their backs, or bottles of reinvigorating juices in their hands… perhaps.

Look down towards the town; look up towards the Monastery, and you can not help but wonder how anyone could have hoped to take the Monastery in a frontal attack from Cassino town, how could any General order his men on such a suicidal task… and yet - they did!

Now, people from afar come by the coach-load to admire the Monastery, its wealth, its history; to stand mesmerized by the views from its balcony and to gaze at the town of Cassino way, way down at the foot of the mountain. But if they were only to close their eyes for a minute they may well see an entirely different side to Mankind: the Monastery in black, in mourning, in thick acrid smoke, in choking cloud of dust. The statue of St. Benedictine in the courtyard still holds out its hand to you but its severed head is lost somewhere, perhaps with the severed heads of

German soldiers half-buried in the rubble, some clothed in church vestments as if to ridicule the holy place they occupied. And would you have the stomach to step down below into the vaults, to pull open the huge drawers there, count the pieces of dead Germans' body parts stored away in them, for there were no other places to put them out of the way, and no time or place to bury them? And those remaining few haggard German soldiers who had poked a stick with a bit of a dirty white cloth on its tip into the open... and the two or three others dying from wounds, hunger, filth, fear... how long could you stand the nauseating, suffocating smell of decomposing human flesh?

But step out into the fresh air again, open your eyes, look north-west... see the white obelisk on that hilltop towering above the deep-green of the surrounding vegetation, its lines sharp against the brilliant blue sky? It pulls me like a magnet... uphill on a stony forest track all the way to the Calvary.

A young man is coming my way down this track... I am lucky – he tells me - for only a week before, this town and these hills were, as at that time in April 1944 – saturated with rain, cold... brutal; today history invites me with brilliant sunshine. But the young man feels lost, his soul is seeking peace and meaning in the history of these hills; God will provide roof over his head and calm his troubled soul. But just one step to my left off the path, a small, strange metal marker at ground level draws my attention; the young man translates aloud: ...*committed suicide on this spot...* *1956*... Suicide! Why? Why here? Had he not found peace in his soul as this young man is seeking; could he no longer live with the memories of the killing that went on here, on this very spot; or was this perhaps his final challenge, his repudiation of the Creator and His creation?

3

"For Your Freedom and Ours"

A hairpin turn further up the track... remnants of an old brick pillar... follow the track for a hundred yards, or so... a stone building... nothing special or interesting about it but a place where, perhaps, I can take a breather, perhaps get a cold drink. A man and a woman come out to meet me; so what if I can't speak Italian - we can communicate in sign language. Gratefully, I cast off my backpack and sit at the table on the terrace. Two scrawny dogs come out for a cuddle and are delighted to have it in English; I get a cold drink, she gets a broom out, lifts an overhanging vine on the wall and uncovers a plaque – *DOMEK DOKTORA...* That's all I could see as the rest was obscured by the vine, but that was enough. Such an insignificant place, you may think, yet it appears on every Polish map of the battle zone, in every story, every book almost.

Doctor's House - *Domek Doktora*

Look around... surely, any activity here would have been spotted by the enemy. To the east, the hill falls away steeply towards Cassino, a clear view of the Monastery and of the distant mountains; to the west – the Calvary - Point 593. This *Domek* was shelled into an almost complete ruin by the Germans but it served as the forward dressing station at the time of the battle. A stream of wounded men from the 3rd DSK attacking Point-593 cascaded in this direction; those that could – walked; those that couldn't - crawled or were brought down on the shoulders of their mates or orderlies; men dead, wounded and some totally disorientated by the battle massed around *Domek Doktora*. Awnings with large red-cross markings covered the ruins, and men with red-cross armbands milling around the *Domek* were visible to the enemy. Thankfully, Germans respected the markings – after all, they too suffered many casualties. Thankfully too, the command centre found a measure of safety in the basements under the ruins, and a rudimentary field kitchen sheltered in the rubble out of enemy sight.

The medics in *Domek Doktora* steeped in blood, shirt sleeves rolled up, helmets cast off, were at the end of their tether with the stress and ceaseless work with the wounded, but how could they stop; they could not rest when...

...*"At times I thought I was dreaming. There was no evident fear in the behaviour of these people, only some kind of fury or madness sometimes powerless, at other times stubbornness, as with this corporal who walked in, stood amongst the wounded and breathed heavily. I was dressing a man with an abdominal wound. I turned my head away from this horrible wound and looked at the corporal. His broad chest was heaving his Thomson gun suspended from his neck. He had a wild look in his eyes, his jaws twitching. In the dimmed lights his face looked aggressive like the head of a hawk... Without saying a word, the corporal turned round and kneeled turning his back to me. Through his torn tunic, I could see a wound in his back the size of two hands. At the base, the bare shoulder blade... I tore open his tunic and uncovered the wound. Automatically, I applied the largest "shell dressing" at my disposal. It covered the wound... He wouldn't let me give him any injections. I told him: you can't be evacuated without an injection. Getting up from his knees, he turned round and said: I am not seeking evacuation, I have to go back. They may kill me but until I have used up all my hand grenades, I will not be evacuated - he said it in a hoarse voice. And he went back... I felt I was suffocating. My tongue and lips were so dry they hurt... I stepped out... in front of the shelter lay eight or nine men... dead."* [1]

Continue walking past the building... hundred and fifty metres... a narrow paddock on the right raised to the level of the terrace, another with pretence to a vegetable patch... two wells side by side, each under a protective hood of stones while a pile of junk protects their back... a large solitary tree in an open space of grass ... and two-three hundred metres further along lies the frontier with dense vegetation. Somewhere there, deep in that vegetation must lie *Mała Miska* and *Duża Miska* [Small Bowl and Big Bowl] where the entire 1st brigade of 3rd DSK was readying to launch the assault on Point-593 and the Monastery, and Albanetta. But there are no tracks, no footpaths now, no Polish banners to show me the way... and the grass is almost knee-high... and that warning about snakes and ticks... it all puts me off walking ahead blindly; surely, it must be easier to reach the "bowls" from Monte Rotunda.

Quite pleased with myself for being sensible for a change, I turn to follow the path of the assault on Calvary. But you can't pass the brick pillar without saying goodbye to that arresting view to the east, so why not sit for a moment on the pile of rocks at its base, rest a little, try eating that cold pizza again, take a sip of water, and wonder why… no… it's not Switzerland, not Austria… it looks too cold even in the heat of Italian summer. And it's nothing like those magnificent woodlands along the General Anders trail I had cycled in Poland – trees tall, strong, proud of the blood spilt by Polish soldiers in defence of their Homeland against the Germans, and then yet again against the "Red Peril". Here, the vegetation is not welcoming, it doesn't want you or any other trespassers, and the Monastery watches you, more foreboding than impressive…

A mass of delicate blue flowers at my feet smile happily at flirtatious insects - what's their name? I don't know, but I have seen the answer on graves in the *Cimitero Inglese* - they are "known unto God". A fly arrives to share my pizza – I hate flies; I am up instantly! Behind me a pile of old tin cans, a mound of rocks pressed into the ground under their own weight, an old fenced-in building under reconstruction… And those two wells! Of course! How dumb of me! Wells - I gave them only a cursory glance… but like bees to the honey-pot, men to the water-well. Water is so scarce on these rocky slopes here that it had to be carried in on the backs of soldiers all the way from the Big Bowl to the men on the frontline… or, in desperation, soldiers went for water to these wells.

In the heat, adrenalin parching their throats, enemy artillery, mortars and machine guns keeping them pinned down for days and nights, soldiers begun to fear thirst more than bullets. With their boots and tin cans wrapped in cloth to smother noise, they approached the wells stealthily at night to get water for their comrades. The enemy knew, and would inundate the area around the wells with mortar and artillery shells - exactly when it was least expected - and all around the approach to the two wells lay dead men, dead mules, fresh and decomposing flesh, unbearable stench... Yet others still kept coming - they had to have water.

And those tin cans behind me? Back in May '44, a pile of them lay within an arm's throw from where I stand now, and many of those who threw them lay dead, their bodies decomposing amongst these rocks here; and those still alive, lived amongst the dead for days... still breathing that putrid air, and blessing the dead for giving them cover from enemy fire. How could they sleep when enemy's artillery, mortars and machineguns constantly belched death in their face; how could they eat or drink in the company of decomposing comrades... the filth, huge rats, fleas and the masses of horrible glistening yellow flies? Many couldn't. The stronger suffered constant headaches and nausea, the weaker couldn't bear it and suffered hallucinations and nervous shock... A platoon from 3rd DSK held the position here; they were the ears and eyes of the battalion waiting for that whistle to blow... so nice and easy - straight up the avenue lined with the limbs of broken and burnt-out trees all the way to Point-593... only that the enemy stood in the way, just twenty five yards ahead, relentless.

And just a little to the east of the brick pillar ran a low, crumbling wall, a part of an old ruined fort... nothing remains of it now, only memories of those horrific events...

"*...The company springs into action at the sound of their officer's command, but at the low wall they are received by a deluge of hand grenades. The Spandaus are chopping them from several directions simultaneously... one man lies shot through the neck... another, from whom a grenade had exploded just a meter away, sprays blood from several places... some men that I couldn't recognize at first slump lifeless on the wall... Some of our men can't take it and pull back some metres. I am overcome with helpless anger at the Spandaus, at the Monastery, at German grenades, at the Germans, at myself, and in the end at the whole world. ...But you must keep your cool... cold, merciless, self control in a fight so personal that one has the impression that this deathly clash follows the age-old traditions – a fight with fangs and claws... A rain of our and German grenades criss-crosses above us. We are gripped by a cold, blind doggedness and irresistible drive to destroy the enemy no matter at what cost...*'*(2)*

"*...From here to the Monastery only 800 metres, Albanetta 400, overlooked from all directions. It's a pit. Huge potholes, uprooted trees, corpses, corpses. You have to run. On tiptoes. Psst. Just a little further ahead – Domek Doktora. Huge rats scavenge the ruins. A cemetery. Here, the 3rd Battalion held the position for 18 days. Others had to be relieved every few days. The Germans opposite, got the Iron Cross if they could hold this position here for six days. In the air above, screeching and flashes*".
"*... They are firing grenade launchers. A dud. Run!*

Corpses. Company nr.2 sits in the midst of this pile of ruins. Germans only 75 metres ahead. See there, those bare rocks... that's Point-593! There are no mines between us and them, only a few hundred of corpses. Americans, British, Indian, Germans. And as from the 12th May, they have been joined by the Poles. Like the waves of the sea, they keep on bouncing off the German sea wall until, finally, it crumbled. The strongest fortifications in Europe, the clenched fist of German might, that's right here, Point-593.'[3]

No trace of this clash of wills remains now, only monuments, cemeteries and fading memories... now, the wells become a curiosity, the panorama becomes beautiful, even the Monastery becomes less daunting.

The Calvary / Point-593

Back on the main track, take the hairpin turn, walk up the avenue now lined with lush vegetation, one final sharp, steep turn, and the white obelisk on top of Point-593 proudly, and now in total silence, recites history:

ZA WOLNOŚĆ NASZĄ I WASZĄ
MY ŻOŁNIERZE POLSCY
ODDALIŚMY
BOGU - DUCHA
ZIEMI WŁOSKIEJ – CIAŁO
A SERCA – POLSCE

[For our freedom and yours / We Polish soldiers / Gave / God – our soul / Italian soil – our bodies / Our hearts – to Poland]

And at its base a plaque and a list of names, names and names of those that paid the price for Your Freedom And Ours:

POLEGLI W ITALI ŻOŁNIERZE 3 DYWIZJI STRZELCÓW KARPACKICH

[Soldiers of the 3rd Carpathian Division who fell in Italy]

At the foot of the monument - an unobstructed panorama. A sheer drop protects it in the south; in turn, Point-593 protects the back of the Monastery, the approaches to the town of Cassino, and dominates the Liri valley; marked simply as Point-593 on battle maps, aptly named the Calvary in the lives of soldiers challenging it. Hold this summit, as the Germans had held it, and you know you are the master of the Monastery and all access routes to it. And it's not standing here in isolation - to its north, from the 1,669-metre peak of Monte Cairo, German observers could clearly see any assault on Point-593, and direct artillery and flanking fire from neighbouring summits on any movement on the road to Calvary. But Point-593 had to be taken at all cost, as the Allied forces had discovered to their grief. How many men had given up their lives or suffered dreadful wounds on the road to this Calvary – 593? Oh… many, many more.

First, the Americans launched an assault on the Cassino massif north of the Monastery in early February 1944. The US 34 Division took Monte Castellane, Monte Maiola and advanced along the

Phantom Ridge and the Snakes Head Ridge; some of their elements got to within 200m. of the Monastery only to be pushed back by German counter attacks. Fighting was very heavy, the weather was atrocious, supplies had to be carried in on the backs of the attacking soldiers, ammunition was running out… and losses on the US side were horrendous. Some of their battalions lost as much as two-thirds of their men. The First Battle for Monte Cassino was lost, men had to be called off.

The New Zealand Corps tried next. The Second Battle started with the destruction of the Monastery. Troops from the 4th Indian Division tried to take Point-593 from the north, moving along the Snakes Head Ridge, but as in the first battle, they were driven off by the Germans; the weather and logistics worked against them, and in spite of the bravery of the men from 1st Royal Sussex Regiment, from the Rajputana Rifles and the Ghurkhas, their effort and sacrifice ended in failure. The second battle was lost too. Again, losses were horrendous.

The New Zealand Corps tried again. The Third Battle for Monte Cassino started with the bombing of the town of Cassino and simultaneous assault on the town of Cassino, on Monte Cassino, and on Point-593. But after heavy and bitter fighting, the third battle, too, ended in failure. Losses were so high that the New Zealand Corps essentially ceased to function as a fighting unit and was soon after disbanded.

But the Allies had no other option at this stage of their advance in Italy. Point-593, Point-569 and

Monte Cassino had to be taken if the massed Allied forces were to break through the Gustav line, open up the Liri Valley and advance on the road to Rome. The Polish 2nd Corps commanded by General Anders was on hand - it had not yet bled enough… give it a chance then?

<u>Polish War Cemetery</u>

On the way down from Point-593 back to the Monastery, the sight of a huge white amphitheatre behind a screen of vegetation surprises by its presence; one Polish, one Italian flag hangs limply at its extremities. Look at it from the side of the Monastery, and you will be forgiven for the mistake, for after all, this is Italy, Rome, the Coliseum… Rows upon rows of places form the auditorium; look closer and you will realize that all have already been taken, all have names, all have a white stone cross or tablet for the back rest, all are waiting in everlasting peace for the performers - for you, for me. In front - a huge open-air stage. People arrive and quickly congregate around the grave in the centre of the stage; they stand to attention; a guitar strings a melody and the sound of *Czerwone Maki Na Monte Cassino*[(4)] fills the auditorium; surreptitiously one or two performers wipe tears off their cheeks. In the old days, when Polish knights-in-armour went into battle, they sang *Boga Rodzico Dziewico*… will *Czerwone Maki* be the new Polish battle hymn?

The singing stops; some visitors continue standing contemplatively over the grave of General Anders while others quickly scatter amongst the graves; some stand a long time by the list of 1051 Polish soldiers killed in the battle for Monte Cassino. Twelve men from my own town – Postawy – lie buried here. But what's in a name, you may wonder…

- Sapper Posłuszny Michał – "obedient" to the call of duty – killed 19/05/1944;
- Brigadier Jastrzębski Jerzy Jan – stepped on a mine – killed 24/04/1944
- Colonel Kurek Wincenty – killed in the second assault on Point-593
- Lieutenant, Surgeon Dr Graber Adam – killed 08/05/1944…

At this last grave your blood could well start boiling, you will clench your teeth rather than shed a tear, for here lies a man who gave his life saving others. His hospital tent and operating table were under a huge awning clearly marked with a huge red cross on white background hugging the side of the Inferno Valley. The Germans could see it clearly from their observation posts, it was at their mercy, they knew it was a hospital, they tolerated it for days until one S.O.B. sent artillery shells right into its midst – two surgeons killed, the chaplain killed, two orderlies killed and several others wounded - the medical operating unit devastated! And now, only the Star of David adorns Dr Graber's grave.

And what's in religion you may wonder – the Star of David, Catholic or Orthodox Cross - they all died for Poland, for "Your Freedom and Ours". Yet you cannot help thinking… there are so few Stars of David here… but there were so many Jews in Poland

– half the population of my town and of so many villages in Kresy. So many Polish Jews had enlisted in the Anders Army in Siberia... they took the oath, yet so many deserted the Army in Palestine to build their own country – Israel. But this one, Dr Graber, like the seventeen others buried alongside him, stayed true to his oath and to his country of birth – until death. But six million or more Jews lie buried in mass graves scattered throughout Kresy, their Star of David drenched in blood... or incinerated to dust in gas chambers by the same German foe that killed Dr Graber. And why? Murdered efficiently, in cold blood... not for Poland, not for Israel but only for being a Jew!

Three men are leaving the cemetery, heads bowed, deep in thought...

Sir, what brings you here - I ask one of the group. "*Hołd, Szacunek, Pamięć*" (homage, respect, remembrance) he answers without hesitation. "*I come here by car, with one or two friends; I've been here three times now*". He walks on, head held high now, back straight... proud of the sacrifice our fathers had made.

And you Madam, what brings you here - I ask a lone, middle aged woman standing by the steps at the entrance to the cemetery. "*Oh I have read so much about the battle here, about the sacrifices our men had made... I don't remember the titles, but one episode sticks in my memory: one soldier took out from his wallet a photograph of his family and said to his colleague "Listen, I know it's my turn today... please take it and give it to my family; tell them where and why*

I died." And you know what, he survived; the man who was to deliver the photograph was killed that day... how unpredictable. I can't stop crying when I think about this. So much blood, so many lives... Oh, and I was so hoping to see masses of red poppies, but there are none around here..."
Overcome by emotion, she sat down on the steps, eyes and cheeks wet with tears.

An old man was studying the long list of names of those who fell in the battle for Monte Cassino; I eavesdropped on their conversation. A boy of perhaps nine or ten standing next to him was asking:

- Dziadzio, dziadzio! [grandpa] What are you thinking... are you crying?
- No Stef, not really... You see, back in 1945/6, I was your age. Up there, higher on the hill – several rows of wooden crosses. Right up on top – the ruins of the huge Benedictine monastery; only a part of one wall was still standing. Down at ground level – the town of Cassino in total ruin. And all around us - a frightening sight. No... I was just thinking...

- Dziadzio, tell me about Monte Cassino.
- Oh it's a long story; it still hurts. When you are older, you may want to read about it; you will need to read about Teheran, Katyn and Yalta, and the politics of war to understand the bitterness in our hearts.

- You see, Germans were clever; they guessed the Allies would land in Italy and go for Rome. They prepared their defences well. Strategically, the best defensive position was here, around Cassino. They fortified their positions along what they called the

Gustav line, and behind it, another line of fortifications they called the Hitler line. They were really clever – brilliant in the way they could cover the entire area with overlapping cross fire from the summits of the surrounding hills. You see, road No. 6 that runs along the Liri valley was the only way the huge mass of Allied forces could cross the Apennines and move on to Rome; and the Germans had it totally covered from the peaks of the hills and mountains here. So if the Allies wanted to push through, they could try a frontal attack along the valley – they had full air superiority - or they could try to take the peaks in an encircling attack, but here they would have to cross River Rapido. The Allies had already launched attacks on Monte Cassino three times. Three times! The first, in January, 1944 was a total disaster for the Americans – they say it was the next worst disaster after Pearl Harbour. The second and third attacks led by the New Zealand Corp also ended in disaster.

The military brass was in shock when the third attempt to take Monte Cassino failed dismally. A cabaret was laid on to distract them from dwelling on this failure, and the Poles, of course, were on the stage too. General Leese, commanding the British 8th Army, was there also, and a silly little fragment of a Polish song somehow lodged in his mind: *malowany pan, malowany wóz, malowane panie do kościoła wiózł* [a toy soldier, a toy cart, took toy ladies to church]. How ridiculous! A thought, like lightening, suddenly flashed through General's mind.

- Get me that Polish General. What's his name… ah yes, Anders… Władysław?

- Sir! I am General Anders.

- Listen Anders. I keep hearing about your "malowane" soldiers, about all this heel-clicking business, this chivalry towards women, about you Poles so wanting to kill Germans. Listen, I have a job for you: take the Calvary, take the Monastery, St. Angelo, Piedimonte. You know the background. Do you want the job?

- Oh yes Sir! Thank you Sir! I will take my soldiers on the road to Calvary, take the Monastery, take Point-575, St. Angelo and Piedimonte, and kill all Germans! And… and get our Homeland back? …Sir..? Sir..?

- Good. And good luck! Oh… and listen Anders: forget the spurs, take some tanks instead of your horses! And one more thing Anders – leave politics alone! I don't want you going round talking of free Poland, of Katyń, of your hatred for Stalin and his duplicity. Remember! Stalin is our friend now! And all this business about fighting "Za Waszą Wolność i Naszą" - cut it out; we have enough politicians here; you are a soldier; your job is to kill Germans. Don't forget, you are part of the British 8th Army now. We fight for the "King and Country"! And don't glare at me like that!

General Leese, bit his tongue just in time, for he was going to add, as Churchill would have said: for the "King and Country… and the Empire"! But he sensed that Anders wouldn't stomach fighting for someone else's Empire.

But General Anders was obliged to inform his superior, General Sosnkowski, the Supreme

Commander of Polish Armed Forces - of the new task he had undertaken.

- Anders! Are you crazy? Have you lost your senses? And now you want to lose the entire Polish armed forces! What are you dreaming of – a golden helmet with white plumes? A Polish General entering the gates of Rome? Don't you know the history? Three attempts to take Monte Cassino: by the US 5th Army, by the British and the best fighters from the Commonwealth and the Colonies, by the outstanding French Expeditionary Force, and you - a miserable, tiny muchomor [toadstool] poking your head through the bloodstained battlefield! You want to do what the entire Allied force here couldn't do; 50,000 casualties – more than you have men in your Corps?

- Sir! With all due respect for your rank Sir, I have given my word! The word of Polish Soldier! Sir, I will take our men on the road to Calvary, take the Monastery, take Albanetta, take St. Angelo and Piedimonte! And kill Germans! No matter at what cost. It's our only chance to recoup the glory of Polish Armed Forces and win our Country back! Remember September 1939... Sir?

But the Germans caught the wind; they could smell blood - Polish blood - they knew it so well from September 1939. They were not stupid; they had to be ready for the Poles; they knew no quarter would be given them now; they knew they had to field the very best the Nazis had against the Poles - nothing less than Hitler's elite paratroops. They tried gimmicks too, anything that might possibly work; and some nearly did! They turned the music on, speakers full blast, and radio "Wanda" taunted the Poles:

Stalin, Stalin, Stalin...
Katyń, Katyń, Katyń...

Stała piękna Polka u płota
A tu do wsi wchodzi ruska piechota
Nie miała się kiedy obrazić
Jak Ruski zaczęli przez płot przelazić

[As a pretty girl stood behind the fence
Russian infantry marched into the village
And before she could take offence
Russian soldiers started scaling the fence]

You see, the Germans knew well that every Pole hated Germans, but the Poles facing them at Monte Cassino were mainly from Kresy - Polish eastern borderlands - now firmly under Stalin's foot, and with the blessing of Mr Churchill and President Roosevelt! They knew Stalin had their families deported to Siberia... Polish officers and intelligentsia murdered in Katyń. Who knows – the Poles just might hate Stalin more than Hitler. Leaflets in Polish were dropped on the Polish lines: *Come on over guys, don't be stupid, don't support Stalin or those that had sold your country... bring this piece of paper with you, it guarantees you will be safe... go back to your families...* And the loudspeakers blared:

Stalin, Katyń... Stalin, Katyń...Stalin...

But General Anders rallied his troops.

Men! It is our Honour and our destiny! Kill or be killed! No longer will Stalin be poisoning the minds of Mr Churchill and President Roosevelt with lies that the Poles runaway from Siberia to suntan belly-up in Palestine instead of fighting alongside the Red Army; that the Poles don't want to fight Germans. No one will call us *"darmozjady"* - lazybones. Go!

I poszli jak zawsze uparci,
Jak zawsze za Anglię *się bić*

[And they went determined as ever / As ever for England to fight]

- Dziadzio, dziadzio! Did you say: *za Anglię się bić?* You mean - *to save England?*
- I did Stef. No, it wasn't a mistake. I told you the difference between what the Brits fought for and what the Poles fought for. Well... of course, it wasn't quite like that, but listen...

So the Poles went into battle; they fought like devils, but at the end of the day, May 12th 1944, they too, like all those before them, came to a grinding halt. A staggering number of them now lay dead or wounded on the battlefield in a deathly embrace with German soldiers, and side-by-side Allied soldiers killed in earlier attempts. Anders had no choice; he had to call them off; and the Poles struggled back to base...

General Anders was in shock. General Leese and others came to commiserate. They had no doubt now that Poles were ready to fight and to die; but if the Poles couldn't dislodge the Germans, who could? Suddenly, General Anders had a revelation; he knew why they had failed. He rallied his men once again - all men: those that survived the first attempt, all the young and all not so young, auxiliaries, transport, even cooks… everyone… including your grandfather who was 44 at the time serving in a transport unit. General Anders spoke briefly - one phrase was enough:

Men… *za Ojczyzne*! For *POLAND*!

Czy widzisz te gruzy na szczycie?
Tam wróg twój się kryje jak szczur!
Musicie, musicie, musicie!
Za kark wziąć i strącić go z chmur!
I poszli szaleni, zażarci,
I poszli zabijać i mścić,
I poszli jak zawsze uparci,
Jak zawsze za honor się bić [4]

[See those ruins on the summit?
Your foe's hiding there like a rat!
Go, get him, get him, get him
By the scruff and out from the clouds.
And they went heedless and fierce
And they went to kill and avenge
And they went determined as ever
As always for honour to fight.]

You know this song Stef; we were singing it by the grave of General Anders. But anyway… the Poles did the road to Calvary – they took Point-593, the

Monastery, Albanetta, St Angelo, Point-575... And the Polish banner flew over the ruins of the Monastery, the British flag alongside. General Leese came over personally to congratulate Anders; congratulations and exalted military decorations were bestowed upon General Anders, and the fame of Polish armed forces spread throughout the world. Only... in all this congratulatory euphoria, Poland – their Homeland the Poles had fought for and died for - was somehow sidelined, forgotten... abandoned by the Allies.

Well... not quite "forgotten" for it was very much discussed by the Big Three at Yalta, and its fate sealed there and then. *Kresy* – that Polish territory to the east of the Curzon line - was handed to Stalin without as much as murmur. Political expediency overcame loyalty and duty; the naivety of the self-confidence of President Roosevelt played into Stalin's hands; the hope of free Poland dashed, and the lives and blood of Polish men shed in Tobruk, in Norwegian fiords, in the Battle of Britain, in France, and finally in Italy at Monte Cassino, Ancona... evaporated into thin air.

You see Stef, political expediency respects no loyalties, it has no friends, remember that! Come on, let's go, the coach is waiting...

As they leave the cemetery I follow them with my eyes, and the huge black letters along the periphery of the semicircular stage of the cemetery come to life – I must pass their message on:

PRZECHODNIU POWIEDZ POLSCE ŻEŚMY POLEGLI WIERNI W JEJ SŁUŻBIE

[If you happen to be passing by, tell Poland we gave up our lives faithful in her service]

Of course, that old man at the Polish War Cemetery did paint a colourful and emotional picture, a theatrical scenario of the drama at Monte Cassino. Of course one would expect more formality and mutual respect at such high-level meetings, but the old man was proud of what the Poles had achieved and at the same time deeply hurt by the outcome of their sacrifice; he wanted to pass this on to his boy in a memorable way.

Inevitably, walking the lines of the one thousand white crosses and seeing that Polish group stand to attention at the sound of "Czerwone Maki" I, too, yielded to emotion - my back straightened, chin thrust forward, and listened aside from the group; but these words... are they not for the living... to bask in the glory of our men buried here? They did not lead our men into battle...

And now I understand. For the Polish soldier, at last the day of reckoning came - it had to come; that's why they survived Stalin's Gulag; that's why they survived the rampant disease on the way to the Polish Army; that's why they had trained so hard; that's why they lived in hope... waiting for the day when they would mete out just retribution for all they had suffered, for what Poland had suffered at the hands of its eternal enemy. They didn't need pep talks or words from their commanding officers, they weren't seeking glory in battle... they carried fresh in their minds pictures of September 1939, of death camps, of mass executions of innocent civilians, of deportations, of forced labour in Germany, of their home towns and villages burnt and bombed out, of their closest and dearest squelched under Nazi boot. This time they will set aside their ideals... *"Za Waszą Wolność i Naszą"*... this time they will fight for Poland... kill or be killed - for Poland, for honour! They all knew well that the only way to a free Poland led through cemeteries, but in the end the 1,051 Polish lives given up here, and the 1,080 Polish graves in the War Cemetery in Loretto, the 1,416 in Bologna and the 429 in the cemetery in Casamassima... was still not enough to secure Poland for the Poles.

The British, Commonwealth and Empire War Cemetery

Everybody in Cassino will direct you to *Cimitero Inglese* - cross the bridge on the Rapido River, continue on the main road, take first left... the cemetery is on your right. Indeed, you can't miss it; the monument at the entrance is reminiscent of the Prince Albert Memorial in London – not the same scale, not as elaborate of course, just the basic shape, yet I instantly think of London. And the grass carpeting the cemetery is perfect: perfectly green, perfectly level, perfectly flat, perfectly cropped... Sir Francis Drake himself might well have chosen this venue to play a game of bowls had it not been for so many graves in the way.

WITHIN THE CEMETERY STAND MONUMENTS WHICH BEAR THE NAMES OF SOLDIERS OF THE BRITISH COMMONWEALTH AND EMPIRE WHO FELL IN THE ASSAULTS UPON THE SHORES OF SICILY AND ITALY OR IN LATER BATTLES TO FREE ITALIAN SOIL AND TO WHOM THE FORTUNE OF WAR DENIED KNOWN AND HONOURED GRAVE. AROUND THEM ARE THE GRAVES OF THEIR COMRADES WHO DIED FIGHTING IN THESE PARTS TO OPEN THE WAY TO ROME AND THE NORTH

Four thousand, two hundred and sixty six graves - 4,266! Tablets stand back-up-straight, line after line, after line in perfect formation as if on military parade – not a millimetre out of line. Men from different parts of the world who had never met in life now lie shoulder to shoulder in death. Men from Essex and Hampshire, from Sussex and Suffolk, from Wales and from Scotland... the Guards, the Artillery men, Engineers, pilots and airmen... men from Ireland, from Canada, from Australia, Africa, New Zealand, India, Nepal... Catholics and Protestants, Jews and Moslems, Hindu and Sikhs... all lie killed by a common cause, and finally at peace with each other too. And 4,000 more servicemen who took part in the Italian campaign but whose graves are not known are commemorated in the Cassino Memorial erected within the cemetery.

And you may be pleasantly surprised to note that in this *Cimitero Inglese* lie the "loved ones" for you will not find any poignant or tender thoughts on any of the graves in the Polish or German or Italian cemetery. Here though, someone in this world – mother or father, brother, sister, wife… loved them, cared for them and still loves and misses them now that they are gone; and they would like the visitor to know that too. Their messages are touching, living flowers at the base of the tablets grow fresh and beautiful:-

"For King and Country / his cheerful smile / his loving face / no one can fill his place"
"To live in hearts we leave behind is not to die"
"Beloved son of Dudley and Margaret Clarke of Barbados British West Indies"
"Gone from us but not forgotten / never shall Thy memory fade. Mum and Dad"
"May the soil of Italy rest lightly upon you / Till we meet / Wife and Children"
"And all the trumpets sounded for him on the other side"
"His love holds memories no one can steal / Death is a heartache no one can heal"
"Loved by the men he led, missed by all who knew him…"
"For wounds like his, Christ is the only cure / and Gospel promises are his by right"

There are a few others who may have been out of reach to those that might have loved or missed them:
"105027 Sepoy, Muhammad Ahsan Usman, Indian Army Ordnance Corps,
19th September 1943 Aged 30"
"11132 Havildar, Mahhamad Khan, 2nd Punjab

Regiment, 18th September 1943"
"16020 Havildar, Har Bhaj Ram, 6thRajputana
Rifles, 19th March 1944, Age 24"

No "Unknown Soldier" lies here, no *Nieznany Żołnierz*
or *Ein Deutsher Soldat…* all those that lie here without
a name on the tablet may not be known to me or you
by their name, but all are well "Known unto God".

A memorable setting with Monte Cassino and the
Monastery in the background, open, peaceful,
relaxing… a young couple spread out their belongings
on the grass and were reading or reciting to each
other – not the prayers for the dead, I would think,
judging by the happy looks on their face.

4

And it happened

After four months of bloody but slow progress on the Cassino front, General Alexander, in command of the campaign in Italy, had decided for one more push, but this time, he was going to engage the enemy along the entire front of 45km. from Acquafondata to the Tyrrhenian Sea, and with the entire force at his disposal. This time it had to work - the Allied forces greatly outnumbered German defenders and had massive superiority in artillery and air force.

And it happened... At 23.00 hrs on the 11th of May 1944 the world around them exploded. The Fourth Battle for Monte Cassino erupted. Who can visualise that moment when at 23.00 hrs precisely, sixteen hundred and more Allied artillery guns opened fire... 1600! And the barrage continued for four hours! Who, you might think, could have survived on the receiving end of such an onslaught?

Today, the sun shines, it's warm, the world is clothed in green, birds sing, butterflies alight on my hand... the nights are calm and warm. How can I imagine Aurora Borealis... in Italy? How can I imagine the wrath of the Devil descending onto earth and the hell that broke loose when the 5th KDP and the 3rd DSK assaulted German positions... the minefields, booby traps, German bunkers and caverns hidden and indistinguishable from the surrounding rocks, and the blind hate and the paralyzing fear gripping the attackers and defenders alike in the midst of death and destruction enveloping them all?

And in this hell, somewhere – was my father! What was passing through his mind in the last few hours before the whistle blew? Was he perhaps like that tough young man at his side, crying, his body shaking as if in the grip of malaria, so evidently ashamed of his state but the fear of death was uncontrollable? Or was my father like some others who ate all their provisions at once for, in their view, no one should go to work or battle on an empty stomach; or like those men who with gravity and professionalism inspected their rifles; or was he sitting on a rock, a photograph on his knee, scribbling his last few words of love and goodbye... or was he just sitting there, head bowed, his rifle between his legs, mind blank, numb, waiting for his fate?

And, when the whistle blew, when he had to race forward through the minefield, when that white line of tape laid by the sappers through the minefield disappeared under mortar fire, when the man in front of him turned into a convulsing lump of red meat, when just a hundred yards ahead of him, the enemy was rushing madly out of the bunkers towards him... when palpable death rushed towards him from amongst the rocks of the Phantom Ridge which he had to take and hold... when his commanding officer was killed, when all communications were cut, when he was facing and seeing death all around him, and yet... he was still alive? Did fear of death give way to a wrath that carried him forward? Had he by then become an automaton - a human killing machine? Would he have taken a German killer a prisoner… or kill him on the spot; would he let himself be taken prisoner… or rather die with his last bullet? And what would I have done; how would I have behaved in his place… would I have been worthy of my father – worthy of Poland?

The task and challenge for the Poles was indeed important to the outcome of the battle - they had to succeed where all previous attempts by the Americans, British and New Zealanders had failed. Some armchair generals argued after the battle and after the War had been won that the Monastery itself had by then perhaps become of lesser significance, it could have been isolated and bypassed, but the enemy firepower had to be drawn away from positions dominating the Liri Valley before the British 8th Army could break through the Gustav and Senger Line, and open the road to Rome – and the Poles did it; and the whole world acknowledged it at the time.

Gardziel - the Tank

Far in the distance, barely visible with the naked eye from Calvary Hill, stands a metal structure in the form of a cross high up on an outcrop; the white and red Polish flag flutters at the very top. Point-575 on the battle charts – yet another monument to Polish sacrifice "In The Name of God-Given and People's Rights for Your Freedom and Ours".

Follow the well-trodden track in that direction – a massive German bunker cut deep into the rock still shocks at the thought of how many lives it must have taken before it itself was taken... a huge artillery emplacement, its guns now gone, but its commanding position still provides a panoramic view of the Liri valley it once dominated and conjures the vision of death it once showered upon Allied forces... and those boulders and rocks on higher ground... how many more German bunkers now lie shattered there?

Eventually, the track levels off and brings you onto a flat area and the ruins of Masseria Albanetta, and you may well wonder why does this place, why this Albanetta so often comes up in the context of the battle for Monte Cassino, and why this obviously cherished small shrine to the Holy Madonna stands here, in this forsaken place? Very little of the farm remains now: one corner of a building in white stone still stands entwined in ivy, a strange barrack stands next to it. Perplexed, you look around: to the east, the white monument on Point-593 is clearly visible; look north-west - that steel lattice cross with the Polish flag, a little further – St Angelo.

Two other tracks lead from Albanetta; follow the one marked *Gardziel*... hot, deathly silence. Up and over a gentle hump... and a strange structure begins to emerge as if from below the ground. At first, it's not even recognizable for what it is, only as you get closer you see the steel tracks of a tank welded rigid into the shape of a cross emerging from within its bowels. Its turret blasted off lies beside it, its machinegun missing... all in a concrete enclosure to protect the tank's soft underbelly – a lesson from El Alamain perhaps. What's so special about this place, why here, why such a strange monument, so insignificant in comparison with the lofty monuments to 5th KDP and 3rd DSK. The tank, so deadly in battle, yet here it looks so small, so pitiful… how could anyone get inside it, or get out? Indeed, how could anyone get out from a burning tank! Many didn't… and a long list of names of men from the Polish armoured brigade killed on the Monte Cassino front follows the heading.

BOHATEROM 4^{go} PUŁKU PANCERNEGO POLEGŁYM W MARSZU DO POLSKI

[To The Heroes of The 4th Polish Armoured Regiment Who Gave Their Lives On Their March to Poland]

On the left - the Phantom Ridge, on the right - Snakes Head Ridge… and the two converge here at *Gardziel* where the tank rests - a gap no more than the width of two tanks, three at most. *Gardzie*l – a frightening word - the throat of a dragon that blasts a tongue of flame at you, and devours your cinder. It straddles and strangles Cavendish Road – the only artery able to bring men, materials and tanks to the battlefront here. Anyone who wants to force *Gardziel* on the way to the Monastery - beware!

The track leading to Albanetta from the far side of *Gardziel* had been densely seeded by the Germans with anti personnel and anti tank mines – a distance of some three hundred metres all the way up to that hump. Nothing could get across it alive - neither tanks nor men; try, and you are blown up on a mine or riddled by bullets as the plaque on the tank spells out.

A US tank squadron had tried in February and its six tanks blew up on mines even before they got close to *Gardziel*. In March, New Zealanders tried to surprise the enemy holding the Monastery by sending tanks up the Cavendish Road – they got as far as *Gardziel* only to get stranded without infantry support and had to back out. Polish armour tried to force *Gardziel* on 12th May. Two squadrons of tanks went in with infantry support; Polish sappers tried to clear the mines in the path for the tanks but couldn't get beyond the hump as they were being picked off one by one by German sharpshooters. They too failed and had to withdraw.

They tried again on the 18th May. In desperation their tanks tried to ride roughshod over the minefield – five were blown up or damaged. A dreadful, impossible task for tanks sitting in a minefield wedged in between German emplacements on the slopes of the Phantom ridge and Snakes Head Ridge and Albanetta facing them head-on. In one final attempt Polish tanks clambered up the steep slope of the Phantom Ridge – seemingly impossible boulders, rocks, fallen trees obstructed their climb, but they went... Only one got through; it stood on the ridge and looked down on Albanetta. German defenders froze in utter shock... but this was no phantom tank - its cannon roared, and German bunkers burst into smithereens; rocks, debris, human bodies flew high into the air... *Gardziel* was forced, Albanetta taken!

And all would have been forgotten, and I would never have known or felt the pain of this place but for that strange, curious tank, that strange cross and the two plaques at its base. The message on the other side of the tank will not let me or you forget those that gave their lives here for our sakes - they will live on:-

TU POLEGLI PIERWSI ŻOŁNIERZE
ODRODZONEJ BRONI PANCERNEJ
12 MAJ 1944
 Lt. Białecki Ludomir
 Corp Ambrożej Eugeniusz
 Corp Bogdajewicz Edward
 Corp Karczewicz Bolesław
 Corp Nickowski Józef

W WALKACH POD MONTE CASSINO
NAD – ADRIATYKIEM - W APENINACH-
POD BOLONIĄ
OD 12 MAJA 1944 DO 21 KWIETNIA 1945
(41 names listed below)
4TH ARMOUR REGIMENT FOR ITS
SOLDIERS

[At this spot fell the first soldiers of the reborn Armoured Brigade 12 May 1944]
[In the battles at Monte Cassino -the Adriatic - in the Apennines - in Bologna
from 12 May 1944 to 21 April 1945]

<u>Colle St Angelo - The Angel of Wrath</u>

A little to the left of the *Gardziel* track, beckons another. A long, arduous track leads up and up and seems to go on for ever until, quite unexpectedly, a single strand of loosely strung barbed wire bars the way; and thank the Lord that it does, for one more step and you would have tumbled down a near-precipice! What a magnificent view though... a big, pale-blue sky hazy in the sun at noon... and the sombre, almost cruel beauty of those cascading and seemingly gentle humps of the Phantom Ridge sparsely covered by stunted shrubs parched grey by the blistering sun. Yet, they draw your soul... you will want to step out, hug them almost, for you know they meant blood and death to so many of our men. Somewhere there, stood *Domek na Widmie* – a house on the Phantom Ridge; German paratroopers had their command centre there; it changed hands many times... it cost our men dearly in lives.

And right at your feet the world drops into a vast void. Half way down, as if to break your fall, lies the village Santa Lucia appearing almost miniscule from this height, lower still, Piedimonte... and then you land on the flatness of the Liri Valley. You could scramble back - if you can - up the thin line of serpentine, up the terraces while the brutal sun is burning you out.

But you can't escape the hypnotic presence of the "Lord of Cassino" – Monte Cairo. He is simply there, dominant but passive - grey, his bald head covered by a white toupee of cloud, seemingly deep in thought and sadness contemplating the perversity and stupidity of Mankind. Tourists from Germany came to visit seventy years ago and stayed... then came their Legions and with them their own Master. They hung out their banners with the black Swastika and saluted their Master like the Romans of old, but the ancient greeting of "hail Caesar" corrupted into "hail

Hitler! They bound the "Lord of Cassino" with the Gustav and the Hitler belt of steel, and like lice on human body, bit deep into his flesh forming pits, caves, and bunkers like scabs or warts of steel, concrete or rock ready to explode with fire.

Later, others came… but this time visitors came from the USA, from Great Britain and her Empire and Dominions, from France, Poland… from all over the world, almost, to set this "Lord" and his people free. And they left me a marker so I, too, can retrace the footsteps of our fathers – that white & red Polish banner painted on the rock just below the strand of barbed wire. So… the Poles were here; that's the path they took. Looking into the void is scary, but now that I know our fathers had been here, I know I must walk this path… not right now… when heat exhaustion eases, when I have recovered my strength, perhaps next time soon, but - I must.

The Valley of Death - Point-575

Retracing my steps from the edge of the void, the path on the right offers a shortcut to Point-575. On the map it looks good - no worse than any other - but it's proving to be pretty awful. For years abandoned to Nature, it is heavily overgrown now; almost impassable in places and only visited by cattle, if at all, it meanders and leads to somewhere quite directionless. Ah… at last a sound of life… a cow's bell rings, and rings again and again… an opening in the dense shrubs… a shelter for cattle and their attendants. But there's no sign of any cattle, no life here… the bell just rings… the wind is its ringer. And whither from here – up or down, left… right, or straight? No signposts here. The sun is high, it casts no shadows; it's not here to guide a visitor but to burn, to scorch. The bell is silent now; deathly silence envelops the world here; a feeling of apprehension and claustrophobia envelops me… and suddenly, I know - I am in *Dolina Śmierci*; I am lost in the Valley of Death!

Our fathers had to run this gauntlet – enemy machinegun fire from St Angelo, from Point-575 and Point-593 on one side of the valley, the Phantom Ridge on the other, and the artillery and mortars… But they won the battle; they knew others will come to retrace their footsteps so they left a marker for me too – here it is! That small Polish banner painted on a stone shows me the way out of this Valley of Death… Oh! What relief! Thank you!

Up and up and up… and before reaching the peak, Nature has put on for the visitor a display replicating what a soldier might well have seen at the time of the battle. Perhaps it was a forest fire, or perhaps the show is just for me, but a vast area on the approach to the peak lies devastated: blackened trees devoid of any leaf or life, ash-covered ground, rocks and boulders like pieces of mountain exploded and strewn alongside the track, and at the summit, nothing but boulders and smashed rock. The dead and military materiel have long been cleared from the battlefield, but you can't miss what's left of German bunkers here. The panoramic view from this point is breathtaking, but had you raised your head at the time of the battle to even take a peep at this marvel, you would have had to pay with your life. It's beyond my imagination how the Poles could have taken the hill... yet they did!

A huge steel-lattice cross mounted on the verge of a precipitous outcrop commemorates the sacrifice of men from the 5th KDP - somewhere there, amongst them, was my father too. As I crane my neck to look at the Polish flag at the very top of the cross, my head spins, my foot trips on the steps... how could anyone have climbed the lattice to plant that flag, itself attached to a long staff! In the freezing conditions of winter and early spring this must have been an impossible place even deep in the bunkers; but today, one wants to linger in the warmth of the sun, to rest, to ponder in solitude why, why... and to contemplate the answer at the foot of the cross:

W IMIE PRAW BOSKICH I LUDZKICH
ZA WOLNOŚĆ WASZĄ I NASZĄ
W SPEŁNIENIU TESTAMENTU PRZODKÓW
JAKO DROGOWSKAZ DLA PRZYSZŁYCH
POKOLEŃ ZA WILNO I LWÓW SYMBOLE
MOCY RZECZYPOSPOLITEJ
WALCZYLI – UMIERALI – ZWYCIĘŻALI

[In the Name of God-given and People's rights
For Your Freedom and Ours
Executing the testament of our forefathers
Setting an example for future generations
For Wilno and Lwów the symbols
of the might of our Commonwealth
Fought – died – vanquished]

Masseria Albanetta

The way down from Point-575 takes you right into the very bottom of the Valley of Death, and again you will nervously stop and argue whether to go left or right or should you follow the track going up or the one going down, for none lead in the direction you would expect... until again, just there, that white-red marker on a stone! So the Poles have been here too and, thankfully, they will guide you out of this hellhole. But that feeling of apprehension and claustrophobia persists until the very end, until you emerge in… Albanetta!

Albanetta – the solar plexus of the German defence system around Cassino. Just look around you – Monte Cassino with its Monastery, Point-593, Point-575, St Angelo, the Phantom Ridge… together they form an integrated German defence system supported by artillery on Passo Corno, and the entire area is read like the palm of your hand by the all-seeing eyes on Monte Cairo. They dominate Albanetta and, in turn, Albanetta dominates the southern slopes of the Phantom Ridge (*Widmo*) and the approach from the north along the Cavendish Road through *Gardziel*. Who would have dared assault such positions? Yet they did…

The sun blisters, the new Albanetta farm stands in solitude surrounded by green meadows, but no flowers, no butterflies, no larks singing in the air, no sound, not a soul in sight. But the shattered ruins of the old *Masseria Albanetta*, that small shrine with the Madonna clothed in wilting blues, that metal junk at her feet, and that barrack or German bunker next to it bring the history of May 1944 to life; it vibrates in my head. A sudden burst of action from within the bunker throws me to one side... one, two, three... ten big brutes rush out of the bunker, pass me, and into the field nearby... no, no, not German paratroopers – white, horned cattle! They stop, turn their questioning eyes on me – what the hell are you doing here; the war is long over? Your father survived! But still I can't shake off thoughts of the carnage, of the nauseating smell in the air, dead and mutilated human bodies strewn in that meadow now taken over by cows, that paralyzing fear or hatred in men's eyes turning them into cold-blooded killing machines, the horrendous noise, smoke, commotion... and in all this the last whispered words of a dying soldier - *za Polske, pomścij mnie*...for Poland, avenge me...

5

And the dead admonish to…

Take the old Caruso road north from the hotel - it's an easy and pleasant walk of four or five kilometres to the village of Caira. The road hugs the steeply rising hills on its left with the mountains of Maiola and D'Onufro almost within arms-length hiding Monte Cassino from view; Monte Rotundo sits a little further along. To the right – the faint sound of flowing water; a plaque proudly announces *Fiume Rapido*! Surely, this can't be right – river Rapido? Was this the same Rapido, the almost insurmountable obstacle at the foot of the Cassino Massive that had cost the Allies hundreds of lives? Why, right now it's nothing more than a ditch along the road. It's hard to imagine that in the winter and early spring of 1944, this same Rapido had flooded the open plain to its left and turned it into quagmire impassable to army trucks and tanks.

In April/May 1944, Polish 2nd Corps was grouping in Acquafondata some 15 miles east of Cassino and just out of reach of enemy artillery. Men and materiel on the way to the front moved down the Inferno Track, then across the Rapido plain to Portella and then the last kilometre or so to Villa or Caira, and on to the front itself. Villa and its old barracks are long gone now, and the sound of Parallel Road, Caruso Road, Clapham Junction… and so many other names deeply impressed in the memories of men taking part in the

Cassino campaign are lost in time and in the noise of the expanding post-war town of Cassino.

Look at this area from the height of Google satellites and a curious shape will draw your attention. A concertina of archways - one, two... seven takes shape, and as you look at it from closer-up... a cemetery! A woman passer-by volunteers to point me in the right direction: *ah, Cimitero Tedesco...?* and motions to follow her; and so I do. Indeed, a signpost directs visitors to *Cimitero Militare Germanico*, and to my great surprise, the garden of a private house along the way is covered in a mass of red poppies.

<u>German War Cemetery in Caira - Cassino</u>

The reception and information pavilion stands adjacent to the entrance; a big, bearded, German-looking Italian welcomes visitors and expounds on the German tragedy here in Cassino. A map on the wall marks the number of German military cemeteries in Italy... here in Cassino - he tells me - 20,000 German soldiers lie in - eternal peace!

Pass the entrance gate, walk up the path, then through the open door into the ante-chamber and... now you know:

20057

DEUTSHE SOLDATEN
SIND AUF DIESEM FRIEDHOF
ZUR LETZTEN RUHE GEBETTET

20,057 German Soldiers lie buried here. Indeed, now you know the German tragedy. In the open-air entrance hall, the sculpture in black bronze will make you stop and wonder - a father patting his son on the back? But their faces are sombre, sad... quite incongruent with a father saying to his son: well done my boy, well done! Is he not perhaps saying: bear up my boy, bear up – you lost your mother and I lost my wife in the Allied bombings of Dresden... and your elder brother here in Cassino? And then you enter a different world...

One, two, three... terraces in the shape of a horse shoe mount the hill, and along the periphery of each terrace stand small, equally spaced vertical tablets with names, rank, DOB and death of German "victims" – three names on each tablet. I happen to look at the names on the nearest tablet and... freeze in shock! Surely, any Pole coming here must feel the same. What's in a name, you may ask – just look at those tablets right at the entrance: Ludwik Woytkowiak, Stefan Surowy, Julius Dominik, Paul Ptak, Walter Groszek, Ewald Raczinski, Alfons Jablonski, Franz Kolednik... These are Polish surnames, through and through! Who were these dead "Polish" soldiers – these German paratroopers, or grenadiers? Were they Polish men Germanized to the extent that they were aiming at the hearts of their brothers or cousins fighting for Poland? Perhaps... but there were many other German soldiers, as the following note from the battlefront shows, who tried to cross over to the Polish lines; many paid for it with their lives...

"German patrol appeared just a few minutes after we had set the trap. When the leading group of about ten Germans came to within about forty metres, we opened fire. It was a

complete surprise; the Germans scattered in total disarray looking for shelter. A number of them fell and lay on the ground... other groups were coming up... firing from automatics... And at this moment several Germans with their hands up started walking directly towards the Polish unit... a Polish voice was heard...   "Don't shoot!" But the explosion of firing drowned the sound of the next sentence that only men closest to them heard: "I already have so many bullets in me... forty men against you..." and he dropped to the ground... He died a little later on a stretcher carried by Polish men."

"...The letters and documents found on his body tell the tragic story of Józef Wejtko, a Pole from Silesia. Conscripted into the German army, he carried the identity of a Category 3 "Volkesdeutsche", a group that according to German directives must be subject to the strictest control and observation. He was recently back from leave at home in Katowice. He had a letter from his mother on him. And in spite of the terror that surrounded him, he was first to walk towards Polish lines with hands raised in the air... His mother wrote: "God keep you safe my son" He fell tragically between the Germans and the Poles, between friends and enemies, in no-man's land – symbolizing the tragedy of the Polish Nation."

"....Four German soldiers crossed over to the Polish side: three Poles, one Yugoslav." [(5)]

Indeed, what a tragic end. Where is Józef Wejtko's final resting place? His heart was with Poland, but there is no place for him amongst the 1051 Polish soldiers buried in Monte Cassino. The Poles took him in but he died wearing a German uniform; the Germans shot him in the back – is there a place for Poles like him in this cemetery, or is his final resting place perhaps only "Known unto God"?

And my two uncles from Wielowieś... what option had they in 1914? They lived in what was then Germany; they were conscripted into Kaiser's army... Kaiser needed both of them to stop French or British bullets in Verdun... they had no choice... their lives were taken, and my grandmother died of broken heart waiting in vain for their return. My father was much younger - too young to be drafted into Kaiser's army; he had a choice, and when the time came he fought the Germans in the 1918 Wielkopolskie Uprising, he fought the Bolsheviks in the 1920 war, he fought the German invader in 1939, he enlisted in the Anders Army; he was always on the right side - he fought for Poland; and he fought the Germans here in Cassino... that's why I am here.

I would so much like to think that all "Polish" men buried here were, like Józef Wejtko, shot in the back by their own ranks while attempting to get across to Polish lines; but how could it be, there were so many incidents of men on the enemy's side speaking perfect Polish breaking into radio conversations between Polish troops.

On the other hand, you would expect Karol's grave – mentioned in another note from the battlefront - to be in a prominent position, but it gets lost amongst the 20,000. He fell on 12.V.1944 leading his platoon in a counterattack on Point-593. In a letter to his mother he proudly wrote:

"Point-593 was important and decisive. In the course of

*12.V.44, two storm groups from our battalion tried to win
it back, on 12.V. at 16.00 I received the order to retake
the hill. At 19.00 hrs. I launched the attack. We went
forward like the devils with me at the head of my platoon,
we forced the enemy's positions in a horrendous rush forward
– I won back the hill in 35 minutes."* [6]

Up and up, and at the very top – another shock! A
huge wooden cross – was it not perhaps brought here
from Poland? A Christian cross in Hitler's cemetery!
Upright, vertical, its arms perfectly balanced…
German paratroopers on one arm, 2nd Polish Corps
on the other. Had the Creator left Mankind to its own
devices, or did He tip the balance in favour of the
Germans in the first three battles for Cassino, and
then changed His mind in favour of the Poles…
didn't both sides plead and pray and profess their
faith with equal sincerity… didn't men of each side
love their neighbour as they loved themselves?
Nobody will ever sing *Czerwone Maki Na Monte Cassino*
here… will German visitors have the effrontery and
audacity to sing *Deutshland, Deutschland uber alles* to the
sound of a brass band?

But as you look around, the equable atmosphere here
overcomes you, all pain and anger evaporates from
your memories and mind, perhaps even your heart.
You could sit, relax, eat a sandwich, have a beer, or
stand and gaze at the quiet, enticing beauty of the
distant mountains shimmering in the blue haze of the
midday sun… perhaps even to forgive and forget …
until you realize that you are actually looking directly
onto the gateway to Cavendish Road – the way that
led the Poles to the battlefield! Indian troops had cut

it into the rocks of the Phantom Ridge, New Zealanders had used it, Polish sappers had broadened it to take tanks. Germans knew it was there and poured artillery shells onto it; casualties amongst Polish sappers were so high that General Anders had its name changed to *Droga Polskich Saperów* - Polish Sappers Road. What the dead German soldiers couldn't quite see and destroy in life, they can now see and monitor from the grave! Have I too been taken in by German subterfuge, charmed by the peaceful and reflective ambience of the cemetery and the beauty of its surroundings? Time to get out!

On the way down, I notice that the tablets on the graves have three names on the reverse face too; almost at a glance the number of dead Germans had doubled... and I have to admit I will not cry over the fact. Definitely time to go! Rush down the steps, past the sculpture, past the entrance hall and the ante-chamber, stop for a moment to read the Memorial board... and I just stand there fixated... trying to take in what I am reading!

"After the Allied landing and the declaration of war by the Italians on Germany on 13th October 1943, fighting broke out for the beach of Salerno, the town and the monastery of Cassino. It lasted until the middle of May 1944. During the fierce fighting for the Monte Cassino Massif, soldiers from many nations lost their lives: Germans, Americans, British, French, Canadians, Poles, Italians, New Zealanders and Indians.

Their graves are testimony to this time of suffering and death. More than 20,000 Germans have been given their final resting place here.

*On 4th May 1965, the site was opened to the public.
The dead of this cemetery admonish to peace."*

And now you know! This whole "business" on the
Monte Cassino Massive is not Germany's fault! In
fact, if the Allied troops had not landed in Salerno, if
Italy had not turned a turncoat and declared war on
Germany occupying its land, if the incorrigible Poles
had not said NO to Hitler, if the rest of the world had
simply given in to his demands… why, there would
have been no need for war, and 20,057 German elite
soldiers would have been still alive and squelching you
under their boots! What had the Germans been
fighting for then? I have asked myself this question
many times, and now it's clear – most certainly not for
this "ridiculous" ideal *"Za Waszą Wolność i Naszą"* or
"For the King and Country" or *"Liberte, Fraternite, Egalite"*,
or for *"Liberty and Justice for all"*. For Hitler - yes! For
the Reich - yes! They were fighting for their Hitler-
given right to rule the world!

But it's the last sentence that makes my blood boil; I
have seen it in the German War Cemetery in Mławka
in Poland too:

"The dead of this cemetery admonish to peace"

It's only the dead Germans that admonish to peace –
and the living Germans? To what do the living
Germans admonish the world? Is the real meaning
perhaps lost in translation? Perhaps it's not *peace*,
perhaps the dead admonish to *revenge*! That's why
there was Bismarck, then WWI, then WW2, and who
knows what next. In 2012, Europe is already on its

knees begging Germany for help! Well… if not by military means… perhaps a peaceful subterfuge will work, perhaps through the control of Europe's economy? And if at times you thought it's right and it's time to "forget and forgive", this memorable line may well admonish you to think again.

With such disrespectful thoughts spinning in my mind, I leave in a hurry; I know now that I, too, must walk the Cavendish Road – *Droga Polskich Saperów.*

And yet, I had to stop, if only for a moment, to take a last look at the cemetery… twenty thousand! That number still spins in my head – 20,057 German men buried here! A colossal number; now, that makes an impact! How "paltry" in comparison, some visitors to Monte Cassino might say, the 1,051 graves look in the Polish Cemetery; what's all the "fuss" then, why has that song - *"Czerwone Maki na Monte Cassino"* - become a second Polish national anthem? Look, the "English" mourn 8,000 men in *Cimitero Inglese*, the French mourn 6,500 in Venafro, the Americans mourn 8,000 in Nettuno near Rome... But who from amongst them knows of the 1,080 Polish graves in Ankona, the 1,416 in Bologna and the 429 in Casamassima?

What is it with the Poles then – did they not have any marketing or PR guile? Couldn't they have gathered all their dead on the Italian front and buried them in one glorious Polish cemetery as the Germans have done… and the "English" and the French and the Americans, and the Italians too? Wouldn't the number - 4000 - Polish lives sacrificed by a nation half the size of the others in the fight "*Za Waszą Wolność i*

Naszą" have made a bigger and more-lasting impact on the Allies, on the world, on history?

It's remarkable how history has become a way of life and death for the Polish people. For the one hundred and fifty years up to 1918 Poland was subjugated by its three big, powerful and rapacious neighbouring empires – Russian, Austro-Hungarian, and German, yet every generation of Poles in this period took up arms in a national uprising against the oppressors – in 1794, 1830, 1863, 1918. The fight was always unequal yet the love of freedom was unquenchable in Polish hearts. Those that perished in the uprisings remained in Polish soil; those that survived were driven out to perish in Siberia; those that escaped with their lives left to continue the fight *"For Your Freedom and Ours"* at the side of other nations, as General Puławski and General Kościuszko had done in the American War of Independence; and the Polish dead were buried on the battlefields where they fell. And they will fight again and again for the freedom of other nations… and bury their dead on the battlefield, just as they did in their fight for the liberation of Italy from Nazism.

Cavendish Road - *Droga Polskich Saperów*

A fine morning in late June promises yet another scorching day… *Monte Rotundo* – Round Mountain – looks more like an artificial mound raised by human hands to commemorate an event and is a useful landmark on the Caira road. It was from here that paths led to the battlefront: one straight up to *Monte Maiola* and the holding positions in the Big Bowl and the Small Bowl, the other led to Cavendish Road. It's a painful reminder that in the euphoria of Polish victory at Monte Cassino, Poland – their Homeland - was somehow forgotten by the Allies, and the name - *Droga Polskich Saperów* - got lost too. You will find this name in Polish hearts, on Polish battle maps, in Polish literature of the time... but nowhere else; even Google's all-seeing eyes only see - Cavendish Road.

A man standing on the balcony of a house perched on *Monte Rotundo* gesticulates in answer to my question: *Monte Maiola... Cassino... Abbazia... Inferno... Polacco...* and points across the mountains. All these are words I want to hear but I am no wiser as to how and where to find *Droga Polskich Saperów*. So I stop an old man pushing a bike, and to my surprise, he speaks good English – the first Italian I had met during my five days here who does! *That mountain, just there, is Monte Maiola – take first left. For Cavendish Road you walk on, then take left...* and he looks at me with evident concern. *You can't go like that... you shouldn't be going alone into the mountains... tuck your trousers into your socks... and you need a sturdy staff... wild dogs up there in the mountains... and put a hat on...* I point to my sturdy walking boots and to the walking poles still in my back pack, but he gives me that one final look as if to say: *well... what can you do with a guy like that*, and rides off on the bike. Pity he was in a hurry.

And so I walk, and now I know why he mentioned dogs. Huge, vicious-looking guard dogs go for me... fortunately they were behind a strong metal fence, but if that hadn't held, what then? My walking poles could deal with smaller dogs, but with these... I cringe at the thought of having to pull my knife on them.

And... ah! Here's the landmark I have been looking for - the medical dressing station in the battle zone, exactly as marked on battle maps. It's in ruins now and heavily overgrown with brambles and vegetation far too deep to wade into. Here and there along the road a *masseria* [farm] but not a soul in sight, all in total silence. Ahead of me and on my left, mountains cut by deep ravines clothed in young, delicate green rise steeply while mule tracks zigzag upwards to somewhere up and over the top of the ridge; somewhere up there must lie the Cavendish Road. Knock on the door of a *masseria* once, and again but louder... some few minutes later an old woman appears and with a smile welcomes this stranger... *Monte Cassino? Next house and turn left, but uno solo... molto pericoloso... due, tre piu sicuro...* Of course, she's right, it's risky going alone, safer to go in two-s or three-s... but who would want to come with me?

And here it is – Cavendish Road / *Droga Polskich Saperów*! Involuntarily, I stop for a moment as if expecting something - an event, a tragedy... to hear that sound of an enemy shell coming... you know this sound so well by now, you heard it hundreds, if not thousand of times... you cringe, force your body into the rocks... and it does fall... just yards ahead of you, and it does explode in a massive flash of fire... just as you knew it would ... and if you are still there, you count one, two, three... five, ten seconds, and run through this horrible mess of men and mules writhing in the dust, the smoke, blood and flying limbs... calls for help, stretchers... utter confusion... before the next enemy shell falls... please, please... not on you! It's dark, it's night... few dare move along this track in daytime... suddenly, you hear the rumble of tanks from behind and... horror... a line of jeeps is rolling down from the heights, gears in high revs screaming... towards one almighty smash-up!

And in March 1944 the third battle for Monte Cassino was raging. Men from the New Zealand Corps were bogged down in the town of Cassino and on frontal approaches to the Monastery. In one last and final attempt to break German resistance, a stealthy right hook of steel and fire power was thrown at the enemy. 15 Shermans, 17 Honey tanks, 3 self-propelled guns moved up the Cavendish Road... anything in their way was pushed aside, or over the edge. Laboriously they made their way up, then down, this narrow ledge – no more than a scar on the cheek of the Phantom Ridge. They reached Albanetta... sure, they knew they were there to pump steel at the enemy but where exactly? Here, it seems, communications had failed - 15 tanks without clear orders, without infantry support... and with the night coming! The enemy quickly overcame their initial shock and rained artillery and mortar fire on them... the tanks had no choice, they had to retreat or be knocked out on the very spot they stood; of the 15 Shermans, only four returned to base, only one Honey retreated intact! [7]

The third battle for Monte Cassino was over. The enemy also had now discovered the open back door to the Monastery and sowed mines on every inch of the narrow pass to Albanetta; no one will get through *Gardziel*, not now. But the Poles were keen to go.

They broadened the track, re-named it *Droga Polskich*

Saperów and when the fourth battle for Monte Cassino erupted on the night of 11/12th May, their tanks rumbled on to take Albanetta… But, no, they couldn't get past *Gardziel*, not past the minefield… not then, not the first time… their tanks, their men remained dead on the battlefield. But they didn't give up, they went again, and on the 16th May they forced *Gardziel*, they took Albanetta!

But my adrenalin is pumping now, excitement spurs me on… past the *Masseria*, up and up the steep track, footstep by footstep… and like a blind man tapping the pavement with his white stick, I send vibrations along the Cavendish Road with my walking poles to warn the vipers that a scared enemy is advancing. But the sun had already spotted this intruder and way up on higher ground, where the woods and shrubs had thinned out, where you are trapped between the hard rock on your right and the soft edge of the weathered track crumbling away into the precipice on your left – it gets you! I am buckling under the weight of my backpack, steaming, leaking grease, short of fuel, overheating… mouth dry; a piece of sun-hot pizza rolls into a solid ball inside my mouth desiccating it even further… all I can eat now is – water.

Rest, rest… lay down the rucksack, sit…and all adrenalin evaporates, mind blanks out, jaw drops, mouth dry, throat in splinters … only my eyes shake me out of this stupor as they feast on the wonderful world unfolding in front of them. You have to come here to see it, to feel it… to dangle your legs over the crumbling ledge and, remarkably, still feel safe. Seemingly miles below my perch, the small town of

Caira nestles quietly in Nature and in the warmth of the sun; a range of high mountains, shrouded in delicate shades of misty blue, silhouette on the horizon; you will forget about the blood, the explosions, the inferno of May 1944 and the heat exhaustion of June 2012. A widening in the road had been cut away in the cliffs to let a vehicle stand aside while others pass, and today it's still there, it's just for you - what a place to sleep overnight and watch the sun rise… and set.

But this charm soon fizzles out and your mind needs to refocus. The track gets lost and begins to crumble under your foot; the precipice gets ever closer to you. You have just trudged past Zone C, and B, and A separated by shallow gullies still wet from recent rains, and you wouldn't have guessed that men from 5th KDP slept on these slopes some 200-300m. above you in Zone *Żbików*. They slept in hollows, or pressed into the rock surface, or behind sangars not daring to move for fear of bringing enemy fire onto themselves. One week, two weeks… in constant readiness and in anticipation of that first whistle that would shock them into battle, into that mad scramble uphill in the middle of the night to take the Phantom Ridge, to be blown up in the minefields, torn apart by enemy artillery and mortars, or to be shot to pieces by frontal and flanking machinegun fire from German bunkers perfectly blended into the terrain. No, not even a hint of this bloody strife remains today; the sun beats down on the battlefield now as it did on May 12th and 18th 1944; only the larks are missing… and no red poppies to caress the head pressed into the ground. Indeed, all niceties about the Cavendish Road suddenly vanish – just like that! High up in the hills, in the middle of nowhere, and with no forewarning, you must take your choice: the path to the left, or to the right! No signposts here, no tracks left by New Zealand or Polish tanks, no Polish banners on rocks either, nothing! Left - and you submerge in a dense thicket going down. Go right - the path is wider, passable but it's going up and in an entirely wrong direction! I could go back, of course, perhaps enough is enough – but that's not on! Phone the museum then – they should know which way to go; they had walked this road with a guide recently… so dial their number… some gibberish in Italian… no connection, no connection… Hell! Look up my GPS… unbelievable! Somehow, I inadvertently turned off the tracking device - I have only the waypoints… Hell! Hell! I've never believed in double jeopardy, nor had ever insured for it in my professional work – but here it is… putting this amateur to test!

Go left boy… but I need a machete to deal with the thicket! Right then? First it's up, then this way and that way, then down… but I plough ahead through the thicket. Those damned vipers and ticks! I wish that bus driver had never told me about them; I have more than enough in my head right now to think about them too! "Be forewarned – be prepared" – rubbish! Be forewarned - be scared! Go boy, go… forget the GPS! And where-the-hell am I now – somewhere in the pits… at the bottom of some round bowl surrounded by high walls of trees and vegetation… could this be the *Mala Miska*… surely not here? Keep going boy, keep going… and suddenly I emerge into the open! Salvation! I have seen this open space; I have seen it and studied it so many times on Google... that tank monument... should be at the far end... that tank should be at the far end... should be... should... but it's not! Impossible, unbelievable! Nobody would have moved the tank! I just don't believe it! Walk up and down the clearing, look left, look right... no, the tank is not there... the tank is simply not there... not there!

I just stand there, totally disorientated, the tank is not there... not there... not there... damned GPS... swirls in my head. And the sun is taking full advantage of me now, it's burning even more mercilessly... throat cinder dry... only half-litre of water left... Something that looks like a track behind the vegetation on my right... O.K. try it... cross the open space and... unbelievable! Another, almost identical open space! And... YES? It's there! I can see it! The tank is there... the tank is there... is there... at the far end! Overpowered with relief I walk over to the tank, pat it gently and sink to my knees in the shade at the foot of the nearby tree. I am on home territory now, I've been here before! I can thumb my nose at the sun now... my remaining half-litre of water transforms into champagne!

In the coolness of the shade, coolness of mind returns, and now I can recall references to First and Second *Gardziel*. First is the *Gardziel* I had just passed but had never spotted it on Google; apparently this is the one that was mined, and the wrecks of American or New Zealand tanks were somewhere there to the left. How could I have missed it on Google!

Though stripped half-naked under the tree, I don't seem to tempt any vipers or ticks. Is Nature kind to me, perhaps even appreciative of my effort... or is it perhaps ashamed of Mankind... of what Man can do to Man? For all traces of what went on here in May 1944 have been rubbed out, painted over in colour-green... all around me green trees, rich vegetation, some almost impenetrable as I have found on my way down. German bunkers, sangars, exploded summits... have all been smoothed out by a coat of trees or by weathering; if it were not for the Monuments on Point-593, 575, for the tank who would have known? But Nature will tell you its story – if you will listen, if you understand its speak. Try a metal detector... and you will hear the ping, ping, ping... you will understand that language. But the Poles had strengthened the Cavendish Road... try digging and the spade or fork will break; try the softer ground, try the fenced-in areas, the battlefield in the densest thicket... you will come to understand the language of the minefields, unexploded shells...

Hotel... I know my way... I was here a month ago... I don't need my GPS to find the Polish War Cemetery, but as I near it, something is not quite as it was - that small metal marker at the place of the suicide – gone? I walk down once, up, down again... no, it's no longer there! A patch of flat surface covered with fresh shingle by the side of the track... I wonder?

A young man passes me on his way to the Polish cemetery and we nod to each other in mute acknowledgement. Later, I am sitting on the bollard in the car park of the Monastery, totally exhausted, constantly drinking water in small but frequent sips… the same young man comes up to me. We shake hands, introduce ourselves and in answer to his questioning eyes, I tell him of my mission "In The Footsteps Of Our Fathers", of my father here in Monte Cassino… And he? He's Polish; he's here to find peace in his heart, to understand, to come to terms… He comes from a small village in north western Poland… he had always had to prove himself, to do better than others… And he's done well, I can see that by the car he drives – a brand new, white BMW… but his life is not right, he is seeking its meaning… he's come here to Cassino, to the Monastery… to come to terms with history and his legacy…

    - *You know… my name is Kleeberger…* he tells me.
    - What! THE Kleeberger – Field Marshall Kleeberger - CO Italian front?
    - *Yes… THE Kleeberger… Albert Kleeberger…*
I will tell you a story. Some ten years ago we wanted to stay at a B&B in a small village on the western coast; I gave the proprietor my passport, he looked at it and gave it back to me saying… there's no room for you here. Surprised, I asked why. He explained: "a man with the same name stayed in this house in 1944 and he left without settling his bill" It was the General. He stopped at this place as they were retreating and, of course, didn't pay.
I have been spending my holidays in Italy at this place for the past ten years… it's the only place where I can relax, find some measure of peace… and now I have come here, for the first time…

    - You know, in my life, men typically in their mid forties reach some kind of a "mid-life" crisis… how old are you – I ask.

-   *Oh, I am 32, I have a baby son…*

- I will give you a lift back to your hotel, but wait a bit, I will first go to the Monastery to look…

Some ten to fifteen minutes later, I see him walking back from the Monastery, slowly, head bowed, pensive…

- I phoned my uncle in Poland and told him of my thoughts and the problem I am having in coming to terms with the Kleeberger legacy… He was angry; You know what he said? "Forget it, life goes on… make the most of it…"

…and the living admonish to forget and live…

6

A "rather pretty grand chateau
from the Rhine Valley"

Piedimonte

It's so easy today – no need to go down the face of
the void - hop onto the 08.30 bus in Cassino and you
could be in Piedimonte in twenty minutes - if you
had bought a ticket in advance; if not, the bus driver
will tell you to get off and take the next bus due "ten
minutes later". So now, with the Euro 1.20 ticket in
your hand, you wait for the next bus - wait ten
minutes, an hour, three hours until, finally, with your
head full of expletives, you return to the bus stop
twenty four hours later. I could have easily walked the
distance!

Nothing particularly pretty or exciting along the four-
mile bus ride – flat. You have just passed Scolastica –
nothing to attract your attention here either; certainly,
if Sherman tanks and artillery were in your way you
would have noticed them, but that is history - May
1944. So you get off in Piedimonte - but if a tank or
an artillery piece had shown its nose just past the bus
stop, it would have come into direct line of fire from
German antitank guns, and become one more wreck
on the way to Rome - that too is history now.

But look up towards the mountains today, and you
can not but smile back at Nature – trees in full bloom

decorate one side of the road, pretty houses, people relaxed, Monte Cairo - the "Lord of Cassino" - in the background is not at all threatening on this sunny morning… indeed, I could live here quite happily!

A road, straight as an arrow points to an ensemble of buildings on top of a small hill; three zigzags leading uphill take you to the heart of Piedimonte. Here, it's not Nature - it's Man who has erased all signs of the sins of Mankind; the town is new, clean, bright, quiet. For visitors like me, there's a straight line of steps from the foot of the mound all the way up to the foot of what once had been the Piedimonte castle. Try counting them – 300? But it's not a castle, there's nothing ancient about Piedimonte now. Viewed from the distance of the bus stop you may think it's a big German-made music box - a rather pretty grand chateau from the Rhine valley on a pediment - press the button, or pull the leaver, and it starts to play. And what a tune it played in May 1944!

If you came here on May 25th 2012, or in 2011, or the 25th May of earlier years, you too would hear music. You would see dignitaries, representatives and townspeople congregate in the square, stand to attention and listen to Italian, American and Polish national anthems, listen to the mournful sound of a solo trumpet, and to speeches… and you may wonder why the gravity, what's the occasion? And you can't miss the tall white obelisk with the pigeon-of-peace alighting on its top; read the plaque, it will tell you… you recognise those words now, you have come to know them so well, you will understand… so the Poles have fought and died here too…

ZA NASZĄ WOLNOŚĆ I WASZĄ
PUŁK 6 PANCERNY DZIECI
LWOWSKICH W DRODZE DO
DALEKIEJ POLSKI I ZAWSZE
WIERNEGO GRODU PRZODKÓW
SWOICH PO PIĘCIODNIOWEJ
CIĘŻKIEJ BITWIE ZDOBYŁ
W DNIU 25 MAJA 1944 ROKU
WZGÓRZE ORAZ MIASTECZKO
PIEDIMONTE SAN GERMANO
PIELGRZYMIE Z OJCZYSTEGO KRAJU
GDY ZATRZYMASZ SIĘ
NA CHWILĘ WZNIEŚ OCZY DO
NIEBA I WESTCHNIJ SZCZERĄ
MODLITWĄ ZA DUSZE BRACI
TWYCH CO W OFIERZE MŁODE
ŻYCIE OJCZYŹNIE ZŁOŻYLI
PRZEKAŻ POTOMNYM ŻE WOLNOŚĆ
NARODU NIE JEST TYLKO
PRAWEM I CHWAŁĄ ŻYWYCH
WOLNOŚĆ NADE WSZYSTKO
JEST TRYUMFEM POLEGLYCH

So, yet again, it's the story of the past two centuries: Polish soldiers sacrificing their lives *"Za Naszą Wolność i Waszą"* – for "Our Freedom and Yours" - on their march to free their Homeland from their eternal enemy – Germany.

Look down to the bottom of the flight of 300 steps... see that statue of a monk with a benevolent smile on his face? And the gesture of his hand – does it not say: peace be with you? That's *San' Amasio* – the Patron Saint of Piedimonte. Look at the votive items at his feet, on his hand, on his neck – the rosaries, the scapulars, the flowers and the farm produce; and look at that child's dress... I do hope he listened to this donor's request, for I too have a granddaughter of about the same age, and I know how painful it must have been for the child's parents; I too would move heaven and earth to secure good health and happy life for my little girl. Townspeople quite evidently hold him in great reverence and, even now, long after the war, they turn to him for help, for peace and forgiveness; surely, he must have listened to many of them - Piedimonte feels a happy, relaxed town.

Just below my feet, a number of terraces cascade down, their vertical faces finished in solid stone; the smooth, asphalted road follows their contours – one, two, three hairpin turns. Can you imagine tanks climbing up this steep hill? Tanks! At every hairpin a tank would have been like a sitting duck stuck in mud or rubble... back and forward, back and forward to make the 180° turn on the verge of a ten-foot drop... what could the tank driver see but a solid ten-foot wall or a void in front of his eyes? And yet, for five days and nights tanks fought their way up towards the castle – Polish tanks. Who else would have tried that - military observers asked themselves after the battle was won. It was all rubble then... boulders, rocks and stones carpeted the pediment... only the void was still there, welcoming any tank or man. Somewhere not far from where I stand today, lay the tank "Morus" precariously balanced on the crest of rubble, and the wreck of "Magnat" from the same tank squadron.

Who would have foreseen the deadly fighting that

erupted here in May 1944. On the 19th, Polish troops were coming off the Cassino battlefield to rest and regroup; they had taken the Monastery, Point-593, Albanetta, Point-575, St Angelo and cleared the enemy from positions overlooking the Cassino end of the road to Rome; the British 8th Army had broken through the Gustav Line and was moving up the Liri valley. For a moment it looked as if the enemy had withdrawn from Piedemonte too… but only for a moment, for if anyone dared to take a step beyond the bus stop where I got off today, they came under devastating antitank gun and machinegun fire. The British 8th Army was taking heavy losses from this flanking fire, so Piedemonte had to be taken, and taken quickly. Surely the Poles had done enough and suffered enough casualties already; the world recognized that, but General Anders had given his word: the Poles will do it – just one day will surely be enough? Everybody seems to have thought so too. The war correspondent from "Toledo Blade" in Ohio reported on 22nd May:

"Poles of the 8th Army burst into Piedimonte on the north side of the Liri valley west of Cassino, and are mopping up Germans"

"mopping up" - if only it were so, for this "music box" sitting at the juncture of the Gustav-Hitler Lines turned out to be a complex mass of vipers' nests! Only after the battle, it became clear just how formidable Piedemonte defences were. Scattered along the forward edge of the defensive zone were numerous armoured pillboxes, Panther tank turrets with underground living quarters for the crews, and the feared mobile antitank guns. Fortunately, the Germans had not had time or resources to staff these defences adequately; even so, a hundred of the enemy could have defended Piedemonte for ten days and more as they had enough food, water and ammunition.

The ruins of the old town itself presented another formidable challenge to the infantry. Buildings had been converted into interlinked defensive positions with well camouflaged machinegun emplacements, and the basements strengthened to provide shelters safe against aerial bombardment. The elevated position of the town provided a clear view of any movement in the field while the entire battle zone around Piedimonte was under observation from the heights of Passo Corno and Monte Cairo. Snipers were well hidden in the ruins and took their toll of the attackers.

With the coming of the night came yet another danger for tanks - tank hunters. These specially trained men would come out in the darkness, crawl through the rubble right up to the tank, attach a magnetic mine to it, or from close range fire a deadly blast from their antitank bazooka. The mere thought of this deadly, invisible enemy sent fear through the minds of tank crews stuck immobile in the night without any infantry support. No rest or sleep for the crew in the night; they had to be all-ears… what else can they do but dismantle the machine gun and install themselves in a shallow pit under the tank, and listen for the faintest of sounds? They got this one! The tank gunner fired a split second before the tank hunter pulled his trigger... and the German was found next morning sprawled in the rubble just a few yards from the tank... 16 notches on the bazooka lying beside him - 16 tanks destroyed! [8]

Perhaps if the Poles had known the reality of Piedemonte defences they would have been less optimistic, less hasty, better prepared and organized. As it was, the first units of infantry moved on Piedimonte on the night of the 19th from the direction of Villa St Lucia but were repelled by Germans. There was no doubt about it now - Germans were in Piedimonte and defending fiercely, so a force was hastily put together under the command of Col. Bobiński to take the town. Supporting tank regiment and artillery were grouped in Scolastica - in full view of Piedimonte and German spotters on Monte Cairo!

Two tank squadrons launched the attack late on the 20th and as they passed the place of today's bus stop they came under accurate fire from German antitank guns – two tanks were destroyed immediately and the third disabled. The other tanks and the artillery launched a massive retaliatory bombardment on the perceived positions of the antitank guns and on the town – it must have been absolute hell in Piedimonte. By the end of the day, with the night approaching and tanks running out of fuel and ammunition, it was obvious: Piedimonte will not be taken in just one day.

The massive congestion of tanks, artillery and the mass of ammunition and fuel on that small plot in Scolastica was as if on show for the Germans, and they responded by a withering artillery bombardment resulting in terrible casualties. The commanding officer of the tank regiment was severely wounded, three other officers and a number of ranks were wounded, and the command and communications centre of the entire group were completely destroyed. And that was just on the opening day and night…

The enemy, taken by surprise by such a determined attack on Piedimonte, sent in additional troops and the battle raged on. It begun to look as if Piedemonte was impossible to take but, on the morning of the 25th - again - the enemy blinked first; the German side was quiet… the enemy had withdrawn from Piedimonte that night. What was initially perceived as a one-day operation lasted 5 nights and 6 days! But finally, here, as at Monte Cassino, the Poles prevailed; the banner of the 6th tank corps fluttered from the highest point.

I wonder whether the Poles had beseeched San' Amasio for help; or did he perhaps turn a deaf ear to the Allies, for the price the Poles had to pay for taking this German "music box" was shockingly high: 5 officers and 30 NCO and ranks killed, 13 officers and 115 NCO and ranks wounded, 8 missing, and 11 tanks destroyed and 17 disabled.

Piedimonte - The Hill

Way up above Piedimonte, on top of the hill to my left, a cross is barely visible in the haze; perhaps somewhere on that hill stood those deadly German antitank guns. So, steadily… up and up… a *masseria* on my left, another *masseria* on the right, a sharp turn to the right, up a long dusty track, terraces of olive groves... and the sun has spotted me again – it's beginning to burn mercilessly!

Somewhere along here stood a red house, and behind it, the antitank guns that destroyed the first two Polish tanks leading the assault on Piedimonte. From this distance and with a clear line of fire, each shot was a sure hit, but they remained in one place just a little too long. Their position was spotted, the house was destroyed by artillery, and the guns silenced. After the battle, one antitank gun was found in the rubble, its dead crew still lying around it, 17 tanks painted on its long barrel – 17 documented kills... Polish, Canadian, British? Somewhere nearby, a perfectly camouflaged bunker and machinegun sprayed death on British troops in the vicinity of today's bus stop, but in the end it too was spotted.[9]

A red house stands here today, on higher ground, not quite derelict, without doors or windows, but still with a touch of Italian grandeur about it. A large cistern of water at its side suggests it is occupied from time to time. What a perfect location, a perfect place to spend the day or night in total seclusion reflecting on the history or the austere beauty of the valley below. Look west from the veranda - Piedimonte lies way below and, further still, the Liri valley and the mountains shimmering in the heat... what a clear line of fire... beware all you at the bus stop!

A small shrine guards the entrance to the red house; a long, sturdy pole forked at one end leans against the wall... thank you! I borrow this "snake-catcher" pole for the rest of my walk; perhaps it's there with visitors like me in mind – thank you again. The terraced olive groves offer some shade and, nearer the top, a bed with metal netting for the mattress invites me to rest; I can imagine how nice it would be to sleep in the open in the coolness of the night... but not just now. Two, three more terraces and I am at the top. A small building that was barely visible from the bus stop sits fenced in on the summit; a cross mounted on its external wall and another on the ridge of the roof, but surprisingly no windows that I can see. A tall wooden cross stands beside it with a brass bell on each arm and a pull-chain to ring them. Surely, it's not here for visitors to stand in awe of the magnificent but austere view of Piedimonte and the Liri valley? It's the San' Amasio chapel according to my map, a place for meditation and prayer in solitude... or was it not a German observation point directing death back in May 1944?

I forgot the sun! And now it's taunting me to walk back in the heat of mid-afternoon. I did make it back to Piedimonte but with only one thought in mind – drink, for no food would pass through my parched throat. Thankfully - a shop! So I barge into it with my back pack and walking poles... in through the door to the living quarters or some other private area... blinded by the darkness inside... very cautiously descend the three steps to the shop-floor. I must have looked like an apparition from hell, for the three or four people inside the shop froze and looked at me in obvious shock. But no apologies or embarrassment entered my head, no *buon giorno*; I could only utter: Polacco, Inglese... milk, Cassino, latte, latte... and, amazingly, they understood! No, I was not an apparition – just another exhausted customer dying of thirst - and they were delighted when I bought a litre of the best - the dearest - milk. One of the customers, a tall, middle-aged man with blond hair and laughing blue eyes was so delighted to meet an *Inglese* that he shouted after me: *latte, latte – milch, milch… Tedeski.* I understood, perhaps guessed right, that he must have learnt the word *milch* - German for milk - from his father, perhaps a German paratrooper taken prisoner on the Gustav or Hitler line…

Back at the bus stop I sat down crumpled on the pavement, waiting. A bus to Cassino..? Perhaps in an hour… perhaps tomorrow… who knows, a local man tells me. So… try hitchhiking then? I did that sixty years ago… so stick your thumb out boy… no, no, not like Caesar Nero – have it pointing up, not down! No… not this car, not this one… not the next… until - salvation! A small black car pulls up! The young man spoke good English but all I could say through my collapsed throat was: thank you, thank you… you have no idea how… but he could see the exhaustion in my face, he understood, and dropped me off at the door of my hotel.

Enough is indeed enough; time to get out of the heat, go home… But there is still the Inferno track to walk, and the Big Bowl and the Phantom Ridge and Passo Corno… and the trek to pay homage to the "Lord of Cassino". Our fathers had walked these paths… and so must I, one day soon.

It is surprising that so little appears about the battle of Piedimonte in the press of the time, in post-war literature or on the internet of today, yet it was an important victory. Perhaps it was less than a salutary example of planning and execution, perhaps it was indeed time for the Polish 2nd Corps to take a break from the fighting – after all, the men had been fighting constantly day and night from the 11th to 25th May and paying dearly for their victories – but it is a salutary demonstration of the courage and determination of the Polish soldier.

The world acknowledged the determination in battle and the readiness of Polish soldiers to sacrifice their lives for "*Bóg, Honor i Ojczyzna*" – for "God, Honour and Homeland" - at the side of the Allies. War correspondents of the western press spoke very highly of the Polish fighting spirit; world politicians bestowed awards and decorations on the Polish commanders; not surprisingly perhaps, as the losses of the 2nd Corps in the battle for Monte Cassino and Piedimonte were shockingly high.

In total, out of roughly 50,000 men in the Polish 2nd Corps, 281 officers and 3,503 NCOs and rank were killed, wounded or unaccounted for in the fighting for Monte Cassino alongside the Allies.[10]

And yet, in the face of this sacrifice, only Stalin - Prime Minister Churchill's and President Roosevelt's great friend had a different perception of Polish sacrifice and achievements. In his view, General Sosnkowski and the Polish Corps in Italy was a band of fascists that didn't want to fight the Germans, who directed the Nation to repress minorities; and Poland would only become great as part of the Soviet Union!

And as improbable as it may seem, the Allies acquiesced to Stalin's views and demands, and at the Victory Parade in London, all from the Allies' side were invited, all were represented except… the men from the Polish 2nd Corps! What better illustration of "political expediency"… Mr Churchill, President Roosevelt – the Pontius Pilate of 1945. And the "cold war" with Stalin was to begin in earnest only one year later! And to win this new war, the enemy of 1939 that took the world five years to vanquish - Germany - was to become our new friend-in-need.

7

The Road to Hell

I must have been about five or six years old when I embarked on my own road to hell. My mother told me so many times... *Stefuś, if you don't stop pulling girls' pigtails – you will go to Hell; Stefuś, if you skive from school – you will go to Hell... if you don't stop fighting - you will go to Hell;* and the priest warned me too. Hell, Hell, Hell... but the little boy would only cringe for a moment and forget his destiny.

My father, in contrast, embarked on THE road to hell; his road was coloured blood-red, charcoal-black, steel-grey, and arctic-white. In 1918, at the age of only eighteen, with a sabre and a rifle he rose up to liberate his Homeland from the Prussians; in 1920 he fought the Bolsheviks and lived through that hell; then came the hell of September 1939 and the hell of Stalin's GULAG camps in Siberia, and now, in May 1944, he stood at the gate to the Inferno Track, the gate to yet another hell - Monte Cassino. This was real hell-on-earth; here the Commandment to "*love thy neighbour*" or "*thou shall not kill*" did not apply - on the contrary.

And Nature knew just how important it was for this old man to walk the Inferno trail - the 25th October 2012 was a glorious, perfect day, perfect for walking to "hell".

Acquafondata

But you wouldn't think of Hell, or hell-on-earth if you happen to be in Acquafondata in Italy – not in this lovely little town perched high in the green hills, warming itself in brilliant sunshine even in this late October. Very few signs of its actual age remain - no antiquities to catch your eye, buildings appear to be post-war. Walk west along its main street… a plaque on one of the buildings announces in Italian:–

UMBERTO DI SAVOIA

Prince of Piemonte, stayed in this house on 4th March 1944 when visiting the troops of the Italian Liberation Brigade, and again on the 4th May 1944 when visiting Polish 2nd Corps commanded by Gen. Anders.

Acquafondata 18th May 2002.

A little further along, a small shrine will inevitably stop you for a moment to appreciate the loving care bestowed by the locals on their patron Saint Emidio… and at the end of the town, just as you decide to turn back, you will be surprised by a small monument mounted by a most unusual-looking cross. Read the message… ah, now you know… so the Poles have been here too.

ŻOŁNIERZOM POLSKIM POLEGŁYM W 1944 ROKU ZA WOLNOŚĆ ICH I NASZEJ OJCZYZNY UCZCZONYM W ACQUAFONDATA, MIEJSCU ICH PIERWSZEGO POGRZEBU TYM ŚWIĘTYM ZNAKIEM KRZYŻA

[In memory of the Polish soldiers killed in the year 1944 / In the fight for the freedom of their and our homeland / Commemorated in Acquafondata, the place of their first burial / By this Holy Cross]

ZJEDNOCZENI PAMIĘCIĄ ICH OFIARY W 50-
CIO LECIE PRZENIESIENAI ICH PROCHÓW
Z POLSKIEGO CMENTARZA WOJENNEGO W
ACQUAFONDATA NA MONTE CASSINO
POLONIA WŁOSKA OBYWATELE
ACQUAFONDATY
ACQUAFONDATA, 18 MAJ 1996

[United in the memory of their sacrifice On the 50-th anniversary of the transfer of their remains from the Polish War Cemetery in Acquafondata to Monte Cassino
The Poles in Italy Citizens of Acquafondata
Acquafondata 18 May 1996]

A local man tells me that back in May 1944, Acquafondata, roughly twenty five kilometres from Cassino, was the point closest to the battlefront where men and trucks could move freely in daylight quite safe from German artillery. Two supply routes led from Acquafondata to the front in Cassino. The Northern track favoured by the New Zealanders ran on higher ground, had more twists and turns and could accommodate two-way truck movement, but it was longer and exposed to German artillery, so all movement on it was at night only. The Inferno Track was a shortcut favoured by the Poles; it was a more treacherous route along the shelf cut into the side of the valley, and followed the twists and turns of the gulley left by the stream diverted by the New Zealanders. It was relatively safe from enemy eyes and shells so traffic moved along it in daytime too, but it could only accommodate traffic in one direction. Passing bays were cut into the walls of the valley and all traffic was strictly controlled by wardens or police. The two tracks joined at Hove Dump and then ran as one to the outlet of the track in Portella. The Polish HQ was based in Acquafondata, and the first casualties on the Cassino front were buried at the cemetery here on the hill. He was ten when the cemetery was moved to Monte Cassino, and remembers it well. But it's time for me to move on too, to start walking the Inferno Track now if I am to get back to Cassino the same day.

Inferno Track / The Road to Hell / *Droga do Piekła*

So, retrace your steps, follow the road downhill to the far end of Acquafondata in the direction of Viticuso and, if you are not actually looking for it, you could easily miss the small board nailed to a post, and an arrow pointing to *Valle Inferno* - Inferno Track - that in May 1944 led to the hell on Monte Cassino. What a lovely entrance to this Inferno. Nature welcomes you with heavy early-morning mist rising slowly to reveal the first frost of the year shimmering in the open meadow and coating scattered rolls of hay silver-black. You can't help but look and marvel. You will want to mark this spot in your memory and on your map so you can return again and again to marvel at the whiteness of the path you tread, at the tender greenery surrounding you, to let the streaming sunlight and fresh air uplift your soul to the very top of the hills hemming in the valley; you will want to come again to camp, to live, to stay… How could this ever have been a road to hell. Was the Devil himself drawing you into a trap? Who in their right mind could have coined such a crazy name for this track – Inferno! Road to hell! *Droga do Piekła*!

It's so easy, so joyful, uplifting at the start of the track. You don't even notice at first the soft white shingle under your feet turning coarse, then rough then slippery then vengeful, but what of it – you are walking in wonderland. And if you continue, Nature will begin to play a game of dodgems with you. On your left, you bump against the steep walls hemming in the Inferno, so bounce off them three or four yards to the right and… wow! A vertical drop of some twenty or thirty feet is quite ready to deliver you into who knows what. But this time Nature saved you from broken ribs or broken neck as young self-seeded trees and shrubs along the ledge alert you and stop you from falling. With Nature seemingly on your side - surely it's safe, so you continue along this narrow shelf cut by man in the face of the valley. The vegetation now embraces you more intimately, pulls your hair, cuts your cheek, entraps your feet, tears at your clothes… but mellow sunrays still somehow manage to penetrate that feeling of mounting claustrophobia, and add mystery to your experience.

And Man too has placed traps to catch unwary trespassers. I stopped just in time - barely a foot in front of me a vertical drop of some twenty feet from the ledge of the concrete weir across the now dry stream to the bottom of the gulley! And there are more such weirs downstream; they do the job of retaining and preventing rain water and molten snow gushing down the ravine and flooding the village at its outlet… and they are equally good at daunting a tourist. But what of it - you spotted the trap in time! And that tumble off the shelf to the bottom of the gulley you took just a little earlier… well, what of it too? Why, it's nothing; just brush off the soil… are you sure you still want to continue down the Inferno? So Nature begins to take you more seriously and places tougher challenges in your path.

The shelf crumbles away into nothing… gingerly you lower yourself into the gulley… you stand small and apprehensive at the foot of yet another vertical 30-foot face of a man-made weir. Masses of uprooted young saplings bar your way… rocks and boulders… crumbling soft banks overgrown with devious vegetation entrap your boots and drag on your clothes… the gulley narrows, twists and turns as if in pain… and you feel that pain in your knees. And oh boy! Just as well you brought a rope with you, for here you will need it to lower yourself down to the gutter below; but you too can cheat a little, find a way around this obstacle on higher ground and gingerly… cautiously… slide back into that gutter. And if you still dare – continue then, but don't count on someone hearing your cell phone, or your pleas for help. You are entirely on your own here, embraced by Nature. And indeed She is beautiful in the autumnal colours of this late-October day, but if it were only to rain… watch out, stay away; it would be more than a challenge – it would be foolhardy to come!

And just here... you have to stop. Dumbfounded you gaze at Nature in the raw... for a huge section of the mountain had detached itself and slid into the gulley - boulders, rocks jagged and sharp as knives, and masses of broken saplings bar your way. Wow... thank the Lord you were not here when this happened... and wow, thank the Lord you are here now to see it! You don't feel threatened or scared, only temporarily immobilized and speechless. Then, as you pick your way through what Nature has stacked against you, you have to turn back again and again to look upon that huge patch of brilliant white on the side of the mountain and the mass of shattered jewels at its feet lit up by sunrays that somehow still get through into this abyss. Now you know - you don't necessarily have to be in love with Nature; She wants you to be in awe of her.

Quite unexpectedly you are descending comfortably on a track of white shingle. The valley is wider now, the sky more open; you are more confident, and with some relief you know you won't get lost now - just follow the track. And indeed, first signs of human habitation appear: broken door frames, old cookers, refuse - typical signs of fly-dumping now guide you back to Mankind at the outlet of the Inferno Track in the village of Portella. Four and half hours, nine and half miles of easy, hard, treacherous, scary, awesome, inspiring... memorable challenge!

Memorable indeed, but it's hard to imagine long trains of jeeps, 3-ton army trucks packed full with men or materials, pack mules in their hundreds, men on foot and on motorbikes moving along this narrow shelf cut into the contorted gulley. Yet day after day, in a daily routine, the entire train carrying men, munitions, fuel and supplies for the front, assembled in Acquafondata and left at dusk for the staging point at Hove Dump. Here everything was unloaded and amassed seemingly safe from the enemy, and empty trucks returned to their starting point. Timing was tight as they had to leave Hove Dump by midnight in order to get back to Acquafondata by dawn, and to clear the way for traffic coming in from the battlefront. Traffic wardens and police were the masters here; they had to keep this entire mass moving to schedule; there was no time to fix broken down vehicles - anything that stumbled along the way had to be unceremoniously pushed off the track.

Hove Dump was sheltered from enemy eyes on Monte Cairo and Cifalco by the walls of the valley, and was the furthest point along the Track thought to be still safe from enemy. A huge and ever-growing amount of munitions, supplies and military materiel needed for the Cassino front was accumulating here rapidly. The enemy knew something was going on there though they didn't know exactly what and where, so artillery shells sailed over the Dump with very few actually landing in the gulley but, as the accumulated materiel grew, it began to invite a tragedy. First, a stray shell landed in the Polish dump of pyrotechnics, and the whole lot went up in one huge firework display for German observers. Soon after, more shells began to land in the gulley; one hit a jeep carrying petrol and the column of black smoke spiralling up in the air invited the enemy. And that was the beginning of the end. More enemy shells began to land amongst the accumulated munitions, and on May 7th the inevitable happened. A German artillery shell landed amongst the stacked ammunition and the entire lot went up in the air – heavy artillery shells, armour piercing shells, and all kinds of smaller calibre ammunition whooshed, whizzed and reverberated in the narrow gulley; flames and smoke engulfed it and turned it into a real inferno… and the Germans kept up their artillery bombardment until the Depot was beyond redemption. From then on, all supply trains were assembled and loaded onto jeeps and mules in Acquafondata and went directly all the way to the front.[11]

Emerging at last unscathed from the Inferno Track, you are almost willing to forgive Man for fly-dumping rubbish on Nature's doorstep, for now the sky is open, the sun is warm, you can breathe… your cell phone works, the village of Portella is at your feet, you are in touch with the world again, with reality. And as you turn west, the reality is silhouetted against the setting sun – the Monastery, high up on Cassino Mountain, stares back at you, cold and dark… just as it did then.

Follow the St. Pasquale Road to Cassino… peace, silence, open fields, abundant shrubbery, men clearing a drainage dyke in preparation for winter… a small roadside shrine stops you for a moment to smile back at the crude painting of the Madonna and Child, and to wonder who in May 1944 would have had even a moment or a thought for her? Cross the small bridge over the Rapido and just beyond, the statue of St Pasquale welcomes and blesses you. Others have been here earlier – four rosaries hang from St Pasquale's arm, a votive plaque *In Memoria Del Caro Pellegro Enzo*, artificial flowers at his feet, and… just me; surprisingly, the large square is empty. But the Rapido is more energetic in October than it was in May or June this year; I can hear it rippling, see it flowing, but this is still not enough to even hint at the impediment it had been in the advance of US and British troops in January-March 1944 - the entire plain flooded, tanks stuck helplessly in the soft soil churned into quagmire, men trying to cross it being torn to pieces by the enemy…

How different it must have all presented itself to the men facing the Monastery in May 1944. In front of them, four kilometres of flat plain riven by artillery shells; any movement here in daylight would be totally at the mercy of German artillery, and yet - they went. Only in darkness they could cross the plain with relatively less danger, but the Germans knew they were there, somewhere, and systematically shelled the plain. With the coming of dusk, men and two thousand heavily laden mules would set out across the plain aiming for the village of Caira at the foot of the Cassino massive. Their path divided behind Monte Rotundo; men from the 3rd DSK carried on to their holding positions in the Big Bowl and the Small Bowl on Monte Maiola, heavy equipment and men from the 5th KDP continued on to Cavendish Road.

Big Bowl, Small Bowl – *Duża Miska, Mała Miska*

But the next day, Nature changed her mind and reverted to her typical October tricks of intermittently drizzling, and enveloped the hills around Cassino in a soft, warm but wet and misty suspension. But how could She stop me now!

Up a steady incline on Monte Maiola, step by step on slippery stones, one hairpin turn, then another... and when you think you are there, a strong metal gate bars your way – *Vietato* - No Entry. But push on the gate and it lets you pass... into a different world. Alice in Wonderland? No, not quite; I am in Nature's wonderland – it's not the Grand Canyon, or Sequoya Park, or like any of the many other marvels, but a huge dimple in Monte Maiola's cheek. Is Nature smiling too? You can't be sure, but in my eyes this place looks unique... mysterious, unsettling, foreboding and, yes - beautiful in this wet and misty autumnal setting... no movement, no sound, no life... only me in the presence of camouflaged history.

Enter along the path at an elevation of 420m. inside this huge natural bowl roughly 550-630m. across its rim; look down - the inner surface covered with a carpet of trees crumbles away steeply to a truncated bottom 50m. below. A stagnant grey cloud hangs above the pit hiding its secrets in dark-green, almost black vegetation. There's no sign of any path ever leading into that pit, and you would need a rope, a machete and a steady foot to descend. Just below, but well out of reach in that vegetation, lies an ammunition box now black and corroded, and who knows what remnants of history might still be found in that murky world below. Look north/north-west, towards the rim of the dimple at 500m. - trees are sparse, masses of rocks on its surface... but look closely, and it's evident they were not there without a purpose – you are looking at the footprints of the battle in May 1944.

The entire 1st Brigade of 3rd DSK sat in the Big Bowl in preparation for the assault on German positions. 1000 men, stacks of ammunition, provisions, water, supplies and whatever else was needed for the assault, was being accumulated here. The Germans knew this, of course, they had occupied the Bowl themselves before they were driven out, so the Bowl and the area up to the frontline was under constant bombardment by enemy mortar and artillery shells; casualties were numerous. Troops had to take cover; all trees were felled to provide timber for shelters, dugouts, sangars... the entire north/northwest surface of the Bowl became one huge area covered with stumps of trees and shelters like man-made molehills.

From the moment they left the Inferno Track at dusk, men had to cross the 4km. wide Rapido valley and run the gauntlet of enemy mortars and artillery... running on the double all the way, burdened by the weight of military gear they had to carry, they barely made it to Caira – some didn't. Then up the steep track on Monte Maiola and to the relative safety of the Big Bowl and the adjacent Small Bowl; by the time they got there they were in a state of total exhaustion, yet they had to immediately start digging-in and building sangars for cover.

Who along the way would not have glanced at those foreboding ruins of the Monastery glaring at them, but who would have had a moment to catch the beauty of the coming dawn? Who at that time would have found this "dimple" enigmatic or beautiful? Who would have dared to stand upright on the bleak shoulder between the Big and the Small Bowl, as I do at the moment and, even for a second, surrender to the absolute silence and the surreal atmosphere permeating this place? I stand here... gaping... the mystery of the Small Bowl in front of me, the impenetrable depth of the Big Bowl behind me; from somewhere here their footprints led to the battlefront. They knew what was down in the pit; they knew the way to *Domek Doktora*, to the frontline... and the job they had to do.

The logistics of supplying the men at the frontline were of crucial importance as everything had to be carried in at night on the backs of mules from depots 10-15km. away. Cypriot muleteers led mule trains of several hundred mules carrying a load of 60-80kg. each, and when they arrived in the Big Bowl they had to be unloaded and sent back immediately as any grouping of men or mules risked multiple casualties from enemy shells. Special detachments of men from each company were organized to unload the mules, repack, and carry on their backs loads of 20-25kg: everything that was needed by their mates in the forward positions at the Doctors' House, on Colle d'Onofrio, and on Mount Maiola facing *Gardziel*. The distance was not great but it was an ordeal for the carriers – first uphill along difficult, meandering paths, then over the crest and into the open under constant observation by the enemy and harassment by mortars and artillery; a distance of one kilometre or a little more in a straight line could well become three or four kilometres and take three hours for the return trip. After four or five such trips in the night these men too were totally exhausted, yet they still had to be ready for that job when the whistle blew...

Come on boy, snap out of this mesmerising silence! Follow the path to your left... and here their footprints disappear washed away by time. Try that trail to the right... who knows what animal or man had left their footprints here... up through the aged undergrowth skirting the rim of the Small Bowl on its east and south, one pinhead turn... two... up to the very top of the crest... and the trail you had hoped will lead to *Domek Doktora* is barred by a loose strand of barbed wire over a low stone wall with trees and shrubbery masking a steep drop on the other side. Of course! I am on the Snake's Head – *Głowa Węża*. It was a perfect place from which to observe and direct the attack on Point-593 and the Monastery... but the Germans knew that too; they wiped the head clean of any shelter or camouflage, and had it under constant surveillance. But observers and feelers had to be kept there... no matter German marksmen, mortars or artillery shells... There's no way forward from here today; only 400m. to *Domek Doktora* but it's a dead-end for you. And how many dead and wounded lay on this viper's head in May 1944?

Listen to a soldier who was there:

> *"...Sure, it's nauseous here, that's true... Soldiers in the dugouts vomit all day, but most of all it's the feelers on "Głowa Węża"; so many killed lie there that for every two of us there are four dead. They say it's worst when a piece of*

iron hits one of them, then it's as if one trod on a puff-ball; such a massive nauseating cloud escapes then that even the most resilient vomit; even rum doesn't help... [12]

Only 400m. to *Domek Doktora*! No footprints, no trails, no Polish banners here to show the way, but retracing my steps along the shoulder, a previously hidden entrance on the other side of the Small Bowl beckons me in - a narrow track down the western face of Mount Maiola leads into the unknown. Gingerly... down the dark tunnel of trees and vegetation... careful now... wet and slippery stones... dripping sky... a glimpse here and there of a solid wall of green on the far side of the deep valley closing in on me like a nut cracker makes me more and more apprehensive. What's at the bottom - the valley of death? The continuous drizzle now and low skies add to a feeling of foreboding but, at last, I emerge into the open at the bottom of the valley. Oh, I have been here before in that intense heat of the last few days of June! I was so relieved at the time to have emerged from that dark world at the outlet of the Cavendish Road that the green wall facing me now was nothing more than just the face of yet another hill. But today, having descended the actual path the men of the 3rd DSK had taken in their advance on *Gardziel*, I am overcome by the threat of the dreaded Phantom Ridge.

The side of the Phantom Ridge facing me now was dense with German bunkers, shelters, machinegun positions all perfectly blended and camouflaged in the rocky terrain. This was no phantom! It was only too real, ready and waiting for anyone crazy, or determined enough to assault it. And the Poles did.

The first *Gardziel* where I emerged today is roughly 100m. wide, and any unwelcome challengers are channelled to its throat – the second *Gardziel* - where the Germans had laid on a hot reception from minefields, machineguns and mortars on Masseria Albanetta, Points- 593 and 575, and Colle St Angelo.

There are no minefields here today, no white tapes; all have been cleared, so I can trespass in safety. But today it's raining, I am hot, all my clothes are wet-through with sweat under my cycling cape… so take them all off, walk bare-chested, naked if you wish, Nature will not take offence. And there, at the far end stands the Tank - my "friend" by now - my Tank! To pat it on the shoulder would be condescending, to say a prayer would take less time than to read the long list of names of those who gave their life *"Za Waszą Wolność i Naszą"* - memorise them then, so their sacrifice shall not be forgotten.

On reflection… *Duża/Mała Miska* or Big/Small Bowl is a poor choice of words in either language. Pestle, as in "Pestle & Mortar" is so much more appropriate. A large/small "Pestle" with German-made mortars of bronze, brass or steel that crush those inside and grind them into dust! Just listen to Jan.

> *"…If anyone was ever to put up a memorial along the trails on the amphitheatre of Mount Maiola, it would have to be a monument to the endurance and will of MULE and MAN. The mules entrained in the wars of man, fell quietly. One night in the Big Bowl, 28 fell. Two others, still fully loaded, stood till the morning like monuments with broken legs… A British Major had tears in his eyes when*

he had to shoot into those loyal, suffering pets. Next to the mules, lay seven dead men... But for the mules, there are limits in war, for men there are none... Groups of soldiers sprint furtively from the Bowl weighed down with stretchers loaded with food, water, ammunition. A shell can land amongst them at any moment, or they could be mowed down by a burst from an automatic rifle. Along the paths, like the stations to human suffering lie the dead still not buried. A wooded area – cemetery - first aid station – an open area – cemetery – a house on higher ground – cemetery – a trail on a rocky slope – dead bodies – three Americans – two Germans – two mules – three Germans, one with a canteen by his side..." [13]

"...Damn. It's those damned mules again! From way up above, the mules and their handlers were coming down at an incredible pace. I pressed myself into the cliff even before their sergeant shouted: Attention! I just stood there gaping at them. Their panniers were empty. And then they were gone. A long-legged English captain was running behind them, or rather walking at a quick pace. As he was passing me, he shouted:
Poles! So you think you will take Monte Cassino? Good luck to you all! My word, I will take my hat off to every Pole I meet in my life if you can do it. [14]

Into the "Void"

I did try again; I faced the "Lord of Cassino" for the second time. He didn't look very friendly this October afternoon, but still, I stepped into the "Void".

Gingerly... one leg, two ... over the strand of barbed wire... careful... place your feet right... mind these

115

treacherous rocks... so glad to have the walking poles... no snakes... follow the narrow path on the face of the Phantom just below its Ridge... follow the Polish banner painted here and there on rocks... and you have to stop, to look, to admire the world... you must take a photograph - one, two... many, for you will never remember... Dare you look into the void? Lean back onto the Phantom... careful... Nature is mesmerising, magnetic... the void yawns open, inviting... come on boy, give's a kiss – of death. And they... they had to descend at night! It would have been suicidal in daylight... they would have been wiped out by artillery from the heights of Passo Corno to the north, and mortars and machineguns from the German positions on St Angelo...

Far behind me now I can see the remains of what must have been a huge German bunker, and there were many more like this one all along that ridge, and many others below them. A watchtower is poking its head above treetops. What a commanding position German defenders had over the entire void and over anything and anyone that moved on the Phantom Ridge, Santa Lucia, Piedimonte!

Wow! Careful... others have been here before – and perished? A huge section of the Phantom's face had slid in a deadly avalanche of rocks and stones. No path across its face, only some loose wire netting... walk on at your peril... upset just one stone, and the rest will come down on your head! You should be descending... should be... but these Polish markers take you on and on and on almost horizontally; the crotch of the valley is so close now...

Hell! This can't be right! This can't be the way down to Villa and Piedimonte! What then - turn back? Ah, here's a path seemingly going down - follow it. Oh hell! The wind must have been raging here - large trees uprooted, here, there… across the track… scramble over one, squeeze underneath another, and you are… on a bleak, wind-swept rib! Way above you – the watchtower and the bunker; right next to you on the left - nothing but a precipice into the void; in front - a bone-crushing shortcut from one terrace to the next through woods and shrubs all the way to the bottom of the void… What a fine spot for abseiling, or suicide!

Keep cool boy! Keep cool! Yes… yes, I know… it's late October, yes it's beginning to drizzle… slippery now… dusk in the mountains… night! You will never make it to St Lucia before dark… keep cool boy… cool! Remember what your wife told you – never rush in the mountains, never hurry… you will be O.K. don't panic, keep your nerve! Well… the Poles didn't get to the Monastery at their first attempt either… so cool it boy, retrace your steps, careful… mind that avalanche… One leg over the barbed wire… now the… and so what that you took another tumble! Get up. Back to the hotel, recover… You will have to come again… but you will do it! You will follow those Polish banners… follow their footprints on the face of the void… down, down to Villa, to Piedimonte!

8

On the bloody doorstep

<u>San Michele</u>

Four, five kilometres southeast of Portella, people of the small village of San Michele will tell you how it was on 15th March 1944. The silver devils of US Strategic Air Force came from over the mountains to the east and dropped bombs on this miniature village! Several villagers killed... how could they have mistaken San Michele for Cassino? But they did!

Or maybe the pilots thought the gun batteries standing on higher ground were German – how could they have known that this was Polish artillery?

A small, rather interesting church stands by the roadside near the centre of the village; it is closed today, and has been so for some time – for renovation. But the people of the village want to remember the Poles who fought and died for their country here. The plaque on the wall says it all.

*KU PAMIĘCI ŻOŁNIERZY POLSKICH
2-GO PUŁKU ARTYLERII LEKKIEJ
POLEGŁYCH W BITWIE O
MONTE CASSINO 1944*

*ALLA MEMORIA DEI SOLDATI POLACCHI
DEL 2. REGGIMENTO DI ARTIGLERIA*

LEGGERA CADUTI NELLA BATTAGLIA DI MONTE CASSINO 1944

[In memory of Polish Soldiers /from the Light Artillery 2nd Brigade / who lost their lives in the battle / for Monte Cassino 1944]

Monte Lungo / Italian War Cemetery

It's not a hard climb; take one, two hairpin bends in your stride and you are at the feet of *La Maddonina* – the Madonna – and there... you stop, not quite spellbound, not quite frozen in place, but your mind is nailed. *La Maddonina's* face... the gesture of her arms, her hands beseeching help, seeking an answer... that feeling of intense pain and hopelessness permeates your soul too. You can't read her lips - you don't need to, for you can read her mind, you feel the question:
O Lord... what is it with them?
My beloved children... what is it with you... why do you bicker, why fight so?

And you rack your brain for an answer, and only hear:
Mankind... Mankind... They have mastered the miracle of turning rainwater into wine, their lands flow with milk and honey, and yet, they will still bicker and fight so...

Your feet feel leaden, but eventually you tear them off the ground; you move. Here the guard rail has gone over the edge... a yawning precipice, grey rocks contorted into un-natural shapes by artillery and mortars, remnants of shelters, bunkers, sangars, scorched trees... typical snapshots of Mankind at war. But step back, follow the 360° panorama - you are on

a battleship of rock stuck in the narrow straits of
Migniano… and the only way forward for the Allies in
December 1943 was to force the straits and silence
the guns on Monte Lungo. To the east and west -
high mountains cast their evil eye, and rained artillery
and mortar shells on troops who tried to slip by;
northwest - Cassino now but 15km. to go; three
kilometres north - only St Pietro Infine bars the way;
look south – the bloody road the Allies had come.
And at ground level, some 60m. below *La Maddonina's*
feet, lies yet another footprint of Mankind at war -
the Italian military cemetery. *O my beloved children…
what is it with you…*

*SACRARE MILITARE DI MONTELUNGO
ANNO 1951*

No flowers here, no messages of love and
remembrance, no words of wisdom, only names and
dates, three per grave under a grey marble slab and
cross. One consolation for them though - "The
Nation Remembers The Glorious Dead Of The
Campaign 1943 – 1945"

*LA PATRIA MEMORE AI GLORIOSI CADUTI
DELLA CAMPAGNA 1943 -1945*

One hundred graves, three names on each, all
perfectly arrayed as on parade, one hundred names on
tablets mounted on the walls of the chapel… all four
hundred and more - died so the Homeland may live.

MORTUI UT PATRIA VIVAT

"O Montelungo, the Golgotha of our men…" sighs the plaque at the feet of *La Maddonina*, but another plaque in a prominent place by the altar proudly displays a congratulatory message to all Italy:

"Telegram received 17th December 1943 from General Clark to General Dapino. I wish to congratulate the officers and soldiers under your command for the success achieved in their attack on Montelungo point 343. This action demonstrates the determination of the Italian soldiers to free their Country from German domination. Determination that will serve as an example for the oppressed people of Europe."

But "…

The night before the attack they crept through the darkness towards the German lines and shouted threats and insults, promising that they would punish the Nazis for 'deserting' Italian troops in the African campaign. Unhappily this tipped off the enemy of the impending attack. Next day the Italians stormed Mount Lungo, and almost reached the top, only to be forced off by a strong German force that were waiting to counter-attack from a favourable position".
"…The brigade was badly shaken by this experience, but they remained in position and later participated in the final capture of Lungo…" [15]

The Italians paid a high price for their audacity – 300 men killed. Monte Lungo was finally taken on the night of 15th/16th by the 142 Infantry Brigade, and at the same time, the 141 Brigade launched their attack on San Pietro Infine. And so that you know what happened here, a remarkable small museum across the road from the cemetery invites you in. Read all about it; admire Man's tools of destruction. Tanks and anti-tank guns, machineguns, artillery pieces, revolving gun turrets... all stand docile for inspection outside – where is their sting now? Touch them, clamber over them – big toys for men and children alike. The only danger you face now is spelt out on a prominent notice – watch out for vipers in the grass!

A small grotto by the roadside gives a hint of how it might have been in January 1944 – not much of it is left now but it could well have saved many a German or Italian life. Today, a small white Madonna shelters in it, pensive, supplicating forgiveness for the sins of God's children – Mankind.

San Pietro Infine

A strange atmosphere permeates San Pietro: late October, wet, wind, not a tourist in sight, no one in sight, no sign of life – only me. You would be forgiven for thinking you are looking at a black & white film-set in a huge outdoor film location. All paraphernalia has already been cleared, all rubbish removed.... but touch it. No... it's not papier-mâché, not polystyrene, not wood - solid masonry in fact... a village in ruins - real cold, grey, wet ruins! Look at the high quality of casements, doorways, walls, even the cobbled alleyways... and the dome of that church! Or that portal smashed and half-buried in the ground... This must have been a rich and flourishing village in its day – why the ruins now? No, it wasn't an earthquake that brought the village down - that artillery piece and the mortar on display in the village square, and that thick wall pierced by artillery or tank shells and pockmarked by bullets give the clue: Man played war games here… for real!

Vietato – No Entry! Thank you for the warning; I will pay attention next time… but now walk through the knee-high wet grass in the courtyard and slip in through the gaping doorway of the Church of St Michael. Its dome still hangs in place, the roof has gone, thick walls and arches somehow still stand… rooms and alcoves to the side, one with a fireplace pockmarked with bullet holes… signs of earlier splendour… drip, drip of rainwater… weird tree roots from somewhere above dangle in a stairway… Yes, you guessed: St Michael died from that German epidemic - RIP Christmas 1943.

Take a moment to reflect; take a seat on that stone bench cut in solid rock now partly destroyed and crumbling away. Old women used to sit on it gossiping, watching life tick away; but there is still room on it for you too – have a pizza, a coke…? What a pity that San Pietro, the village Saint and protector, couldn't save the village from its primary sin: it stood on the way to Rome - Germans were holed-up in it; the US 5th Army wanted it.

That initial impression of a film-set evaporates – you are looking at what Man has done to Man and, quite evidently, Nature is ashamed of Mankind, She is taking over this place into her embrace of vigorous vegetation. Huge roots, three-four inches thick run inside some solid walls and split them apart in a creepy and intimidating living glimpse of her power.

The entire body and the scalp of the "film-set" is covered with lush green vegetation, and even inside of what once had been a bread oven, a young seedling wants to take it over now... but no, Man wants to preserve this exhibit as if this will help him learn the lessons that had eluded him for millennia.

The Germans knew the Allies would have to come this way on their way to Rome, and they prepared their defences well; the Allies knew it too, and they knew it wasn't going to be easy. A panoramic view from the heights of the village commanded the approach to Route 6, and German observers sitting on top of the 1200m. high Sammucro [*Monte Sambucaro*] at its back could see any movement of Allied forces here and direct artillery fire against them. The 142 Regiment of the 36th US Division tried and tried again to take San Pietro but German defences held. An assault by 16 tanks also ended in failure and many casualties. But finally, *Monte Sambucaro* was taken by US-Canadian Special Forces, and when Monte Lungo fell on 15 December, Germans pulled back from San Pietro to their defensive positions along the Gustav Line. The village of San Pietro was destroyed in just a few days, but no Man could rebuild it in the proverbial forty days, so it was left abandoned, for all to see as - *PARCO DELLA MEMORIA STORICA SAN PIETRO INFINE*

So now you can walk freely and safely on the cobbled alleyways of *Parco della Memoria Storica* but without even a hint of the killing that took place here - no smoke or fire, no nauseating smell in your nostrils, no blood, no thunder, no bursting shells... all rubble cleared now, no danger to you or me. Will it not remain just another film-set, another tourist attraction? What will Man take away with him from visiting this exhibit – a few photographs, a prayer perhaps… isn't that all?

If the Germans had not pulled out from San Pietro but fought to the bitter end, it would have been a costly prize to take. The caverns and cellars under the buildings of the village are massive and extensive, quite evidently artillery bombardment by the Allies did not destroy them; and now they yawn with emptiness and darkness haunting ones imagination, but at the time of the battle they would have provided a perfect protection for German troops, for machinegun positions, for sharpshooters.

But one cavern in particular is remarkable; it must have been used by the German soldiers as the manger in their Christmas festivities, and it has survived almost untouched by the mayhem that surrounded it - perhaps it was San Pietro or St Michael who shielded the Holy Family from the bombardment by the Allied forces? Joseph and Mary still stand in the cavern today as they might have stood here in December 1943, heads bowed, arms tenderly outstretched towards where the crib once stood, Mary's fingers wrenched as if tortured by the Gestapo, the German-yellow of their robes now faded, cloth torn in places. But all the cattle and sheep are gone - requisitioned to feed German paratroopers perhaps? And the shepherds are gone too - to work in munitions factories in Germany? Only the Bethlehem Star managed to escape the Germans and found safety on

US jeeps, trucks and tanks; and one of the Three Wise Kings survived - Victor Emmanuel III of Italy – but he had to accept his German Overlord. And where is the little Jesus - gone to save the Mankind for the second time?

Sant' Angelo in Theodice

It's not very far from Cassino railway station to Sant' Angelo – pass the "English" War Cemetery, follow the signs to S. Angelo… a little over seven kilometres along a good road - one and half hour walk? Flat, open terrain, lush green colours still prominent this late October, strikingly rich, black soil of recently ploughed fields, a bridge over a stream, and there's another... No high-rises here, only a few buildings along the way – some industrial, some agricultural – all dominated by the Monastery on Monte Cassino to the north, and Mount Trocchio a little to the east of the road, both almost within reach, certainly easily within reach of German machine-guns, mortar and artillery.

And standing forlorn in this open space, facing the Monastery not quite three kilometres distant – a monument. A small wooden cross with faded red poppy, such as found on Armistice Day at Westminster Abbey, still rests at its base. The brass plaque on the marble slab reads:

THE BEDFORDSHIRE AND
HERTFORDSHIRE REGIMENT
TO COMMEMORATE THE GALLANTRY
AND SACRIFICE OF ALL RANKS OF

THE 2ND BATTALION
THE BEDFORDSHIRE AND
HERTFORDSHIRE REGIMENT
WHO FOUGHT IN THE BATTLE OF
CASSINO 1944
AND IN MEMEORY OF ALL THE
MEMBERS OF THE REGIMENT WHO
GAVE THEIR LIVES IN ITALY

But search the internet, look through published books on the subject... and the Bedfordshire and Hertfordshire Regiment hardly appears in the history of the battles for Monte Cassino; if not for this Monument I would have simply walked by oblivious. Yet on the 11/12th May 1944 - the fourth battle for Monte Cassino – the 2nd Battalion was the first to get across the Rapido River north of Sant' Angelo and they held a small perimeter on the German side against fierce German counter attacks. They were decimated but still held the ground thereby giving the 28th Regiment of the British 4th Division a chance to construct a temporary bridge at a point across the river some ninety metres behind the Monument, strong enough to take tanks. In some ways this – "Amazon" – bridge was the turning point in the battle for the opening of the Liri Valley, for once tanks had crossed the river, the Germans abandoned Sant' Angelo and started retreating to their next line of strongholds along the Gustav Line.[16]

It's not much further to Sant' Angelo now... up the hill... town square overlooking the river and the open, flat, green land at its feet. A small obelisk in pinkish marble stands tucked away in one corner of the square; no flags on the flagpoles here today, but the message on the obelisk is permanent, and that big letter "T" set in a stylized arrowhead at the top must, surely, stand for Texas.

36th
INFANTRY DIVISION
UNITED STATES
OF
AMERICA
TRUSTING GOD
THEY FOUGHT
AND DIED FOR
LIBERTY
1943 - 1945

Two portraits that must have been placed quite recently at the foot of the column, show just how young these soldiers had been when they gave their lives for the liberty of others.

Follow the road a little further, turn left, then down hill and the bridge over the river is just there – *Gari, Fume delle quattro battaglie* [the river of four battles] announces the plaque by the bridge. The town's emblem on the plaque looks very much like a beetle; and had the ancient Egyptians been asked, they would have told the US Generals of the day: cross the path of a beetle at the peril of death and destruction, and so it turned out to be. And on the far side, stands yet another, most unusual monument – a group of three in fact. The big "Bell of Peace" is arresting and impressive. Set in a strong frame it apparently tolls every day at 17.30 - thirty rings send a grateful message from Italian people to the world that

THE SUN SHINES AGAIN
CASSINO AND ITALY WITH GRATITUDE
AND DEVOTION HONOUR THE FALLEN
FOR ITS FREEDOM
January 1944 – Sant' Angelo in Theodice Cassino

The poem "HO BELL OF PEACE" by Severino de Santis captures the theme in Italian and English translation.

HO BELL OF PEACE
MELTED TO HONOUR THOSE WHO PERISHED FOR THE SACRIFICE OF OUR LIBERTY AND SO THE SACRIFICE OF......

A smaller version of the "Bell of Peace" stands nearby and, next to it, a memorial to the 100th Infantry Battalion of the 34th Division of the US 5th Army in the 2nd World War presented by the Municipality of Biffontaine, in Vosges, France:-

A LA MEMOIRE ET L'HONNEUR
POUR LES HOMMES DU 100eme
BATAILLON D'INFANTERIE
34eme DIVISION D'INFANTERIE
ARMEE DES ETATS-UNIS
5eme ARMEE ALLIEES
2eme GUERRE MONDIALE

Back in 1943/4, US 5th Army under General Mark Clark had a much longer journey, and fighting all the way – first Salerno then Naples, and then here. The entrance to the Liri Valley and the road to Rome was straight ahead... only the river Gari-Rapido and that small town Cassino was in the way. Who would have then thought that when this was all over, those that survived will be putting up monuments to those that gave up their lives right here. River Gari/Rapido flows fast, its banks steep, not easily fordable; boats and bridges were essential to get the infantry and tanks across. The approach to the river was across flat land cleared of all vegetation, sown with mines, under constant observation by the Germans from the heights on both sides of the valley and from the village of Sant' Angelo standing on a bluff four metres above the river. And what's on the other side of the river – who knew for sure? Surely, it would have been suicidal to attack across the river in daytime.

But the German Winter Line of defences had just been cracked – Monte Lungo taken, San Pietro Infine taken, Monte Trocchio abandoned by the Germans without even a fight. So... let's go boys! The push came from up high, from Mr. Churchill, from Marshall Alexander, from General Mark Clark in command of the US 5th Army. Go boys! Jump over the Gari, take Cassino, go up the Liri Valley... and we will surprise, shock & awe Kesselring and Hitler by landing our forces at Anzio. So go boys, go! Smash through the Gustav Line. We want Rome! The 36th US Infantry Division will spearhead the attack – who else, they wear the spearhead on their shoulder patch. US 141 Regiment will make two crossings north of Sant' Angelo and US 143 Reg. will make two crossings downstream of the town; go!

Indeed, "the sun shines again", warm, green, open skies, quiet… river Gari (Rapido) sparkles and ripples happily south under the bridge, people go about their daily business without urgency, without fear… but the night of the 20th January 1944 was absolutely foul. The ground was wet and muddy from rain, men had to lug heavy boats some two kilometres from the staging area to the river, vehicles got stuck in the mud, engineers couldn't get heavy equipment and Bailey bridges up to the river, tanks sank in the soft terrain, and on top of all that, heavy fog came down and blanketed the entire area. Men couldn't see a yard in front, they got confused, lost, communications failed, but they went into battle… and the Germans were ready for them. Minefields on the approach to the river, mines on the other side, barbed wire, dugouts, machinegun nests, tanks, German mortars and artillery zeroed in on strategic points.

But the GIs went. The white tapes through the minefields were destroyed by enemy mortars and artillery, boats and dinghies were shot up even before they were floated; some were launched only to be sunk while crossing. Men weighed down by their military gear didn't have a chance in the freezing water… they drowned helpless, their bodies floating downstream piling up at the bridges their mates were trying to construct. With the freezing fog came utter confusion on the battlefield. Those that did get across were pinned down by horrendous enemy fire from all directions, some cowered in ditches or fox holes day and night… some tried to get back to their own side but the pontoons, footbridges and boats were all shot up, cutting the way back and making it impossible for any reinforcements to reach them. And when daylight came, Germans knew exactly where the GIs were, and rained fire on them. Bravery was not enough; reinforcements, ammunition, communications with the command, tanks, anti-tank guns were needed but not forthcoming. Some tried to withdraw, get back across the river, but the orders came back – attack, attack. And the massacre continued the second day. Some units advanced 1000m. into enemy territory only to be cut off and cut up… and by the end of 22nd January, American fire died west of the river… only forty GIs returned, the others were killed, wounded or taken prisoner. [17]

The result of the battle at Sant' Angelo was a shock and was seen by many as a total disaster. General Mark Clark states in his memoir *"I maintain that it is essential that I make the attack [across the Rapido], expecting heavy losses, in order to hold all the German troops on my front and draw more to it, thereby clearing the way for "Shingle" [Anzio landing]"* [18] But the casualties at Sant' Angelo may have surprised even the General. According to the findings of the War Department, the 36th Division reported 155 killed, 1052 wounded, and 921 missing.[19] The 34th Infantry Division also taking part in this action suffered 2066 casualties – in just 48 hours!

When entire companies that went across the river were, literally, decimated, it's not surprising that men from the 36th Division felt bitter and wanted to hold General Clark to account. Only two Congressional investigations into the conduct of war were conducted: one about Pearl Harbour disaster, and the other, investigation of the Rapido River failure. The Congressional committee accepted the official War Department report on the battle which found *"… that the action to which the Thirty-sixth Division was committed was a necessary one, and that General Clark exercised sound judgement in planning it and in ordering it…."* [20] Perhaps the conclusion is not surprising perhaps for, after all, General Clark was by then the American "Conqueror of Rome".

If you happened to have turned left before you had reached the village square and then walked all the way down the side road… you would have come face to face with the river – perhaps twenty metres wide, flowing fast between soggy banks, steeply rising escarpment at your back, a flat green expanse on the other side. Would you have dared swim across… and in total darkness, and in fog so thick you couldn't see a yard in front of you? And with the enemy entrenched in the village on the escarpment looking down their machinegun barrels straight at you…would you have dared to cross? Would you have said "Yes Sir" and advanced regardless… or would you swear under your breath at your commanding Generals for sending you to sure death, but still, clench your teeth… and go?

US 100 Battalion of the 34th Division

At first glance the monument to the 100 Battalion, in French, looks misplaced here in Sant' Angelo; intriguing that people from Biffontaine, a small town in the Vosges region in France, should have put up a memorial to the Battalion here.

The 100 Battalion was a separate entity formed entirely from Nisei - young second generation American-Japanese. Perhaps not surprisingly, immediately after Pearl Harbour, anyone in the USA of Japanese descent was subject to prejudice and hatred, and considered a risk to national security. Some 100,000 American-Japanese were forcibly relocated to camps surrounded by barbed wire, gun towers and guards with orders to shoot anyone trying to escape. This attitude was especially strong on the mainland; it was somewhat more understanding in Hawaii itself. The Nisei, however, felt very strong loyalty to their new Homeland and publically voiced their desire to fight for America. In May 1942 the Hawaiian Provisional Battalion was formed as a separate fighting unit, and was later re-designated the 100 US Battalion.[21]

Perhaps not surprisingly too, the loyalty of the 100 Battalion of some 1300 men was continually being tested – it seems that wherever the going was exceptionally tough, the risks to life exceptionally great, the 100th was sent... and the Battalion covered itself in glory on the battlefronts in Italy. It sustained enormous casualties but managed to preserve its uniqueness by essentially all replenishments coming from young Nisei in Hawaii.

The Battalion didn't actually fight here in Sant' Angelo, but a few days later they attempted crossing the Rapido river just a few miles upstream near the village of Caira and Monte Rotundo; they fought bravely and sustained very heavy losses. The Battalion also fought in France; it liberated the village of

Biffontaine where they demonstrated absolute courage, determination, physical and mental endurance that has gone into the history of the battles on the Italian and French front. The French people of Biffontaine have not forgotten their liberation by the 100 Battalion and expressed their appreciation by funding the Monument here.

9

"Green on Green"

<u>Venafro</u>

If you let your attention be hijacked by the history of the old part of town, you could easily miss a plaque on yet another yellow-coloured wall. Unsurprisingly, it's in Italian, but you won't have a problem with its meaning:

15 MARCH 1944
BY TRAGIC ERROR OUR CITY, BEING
ON THE FRONTLINE, WAS SUBJECTED
TO A TERRIBLE BOMBARDMENT FROM AIR
THAT SOWED DEATH AND DESTRUCTION.

THE CIVIC ADMINISTRATION
FOR PERPETUAL RECORD CONSECRATES
THIS MARBLE PLAQUE IN THE MEMORY OF
ALL THE UNKNOWN VICTIMS.
15 MARCH 1985

"…subjected to a terrible bombardment from air". Ah… the Ides of March 1944 - the day the US Air Force bombers euphemistically named the "Liberators" almost wiped the town of Cassino off the surface of the world; their flight path took them directly over Venafro. How many times have you heard of "blue on blue" or "green on green" or "friendly fire" in the context of the war in Iraq or

Afghanistan of 2010? So what's in a colour you may ask – death and destruction of people on your own side! Just another mistake! Bomb bays on the leading Liberator apparently opened by mistake or due to malfunction, and bombs fell on Venafro. Bombardiers on the following planes followed their leader and more sticks of heavy bombs sowed death and destruction amongst the people below; and who remembers now exactly how many civilians were killed - some say 150! One hospital destroyed, the HQ of the French Expeditionary Corps (FEC) bombed, the command post of the US 504th Parachute Combat Team bombed; some say 57 Allied soldiers and friendly civilians killed and 180 wounded.

Look up and you cringe a little, for the age-old *Torre Mercato* – the Market Tower – is just across the street, and its crumbling battlements held in place by the roots of vegetation threaten to bomb you out of this world. And curtains in the windows? Somebody actually lives or occupies the place!

Mort pour La France

But forget the Market Tower and the near-by Pandone Castle dating from the 14th century; walk along highway 85 in the direction of Isernia… A man of distinctly Arab features standing in a garage forecourt smiles and waves… yes, the French… no, no, the Algerian cemetery is just there, ahead, to your left.

Indeed, a vast area. You can see the white of the mass of crosses percolating through the trees; only steel railings and a dry moat stop you from going amongst the graves to read the names and the purpose of men's sacrifice... and the steel entrance gate locks you out! The cemetery is closed to visitors! Why, of all the days in the week, close the cemetery on Sundays? Some way behind the steel bars you can see a Christian chapel standing side by side in harmony with a Moslem minaret mounted by a quarter-moon, With a telephoto lens you can read on the graves: *Mort Pour La France* – gave up their lives for France... Tunisians, Moroccans, Algerians died for France! And only ten years later, 1954-61, those that survived the battles in Italy, fought the French colonists in Algeria - they wanted Algeria for Algerians – not for France, not even for Algerian-born French - the *Pied Noir*, and certainly not for General de Gaulle. A large slab on the ground explains in French:

"French Military Cemetery
Engaged on the side of the Allied forces for the liberation of Europe from the Nazi dictatorship the French Expeditionary Force under the command of General Juin landed at Naples on 23 September 1943 already liberated in September by the American Army under General Clark.

The front had stabilized along the rivers Garigliano and Sangro and on the Abruzzo massive where the Germans were entrenched behind the "Gustav Line"

As of 16th December the Second Moroccan Infantry Division under General Dody moved into position following other units of volunteers recruited from North Africa.

In the freezing conditions of winter, relentless combat began for the possession of Monte Cassino. At last, on the 18th May, thanks to the audacious manoeuvre by General Juin in the Aurunchi mountains, the bolt shot, opens the road to Rome (4 June 1944). Numbering 15,000 in December 1943, 113,000 in May 1944, French troops had suffered 6,577 killed, 2,088 missing and 23,506 wounded.

The cemetery in Venafro inters soldiers killed in the battle for the "Gustav Line" and includes those who died in the hospitals in Naples and initially were buried in 4922 temporary graves.

Passers-by please bear in mind that our freedom has been paid for with their blood."

6,577 killed, 23,500 wounded! The Free French headed by General de Gaulle had a good reason to fight alongside the British and Americans - they fought and died to erase the ignominy of the Vichy Government and to restore the glory of French arms after the collapse of their armies in 1940; they fought for the honour of France. But in 1943 the French Army in North Africa was still under the Vichy government, so whose side would they be on when Allied forces land in Algeria to embark on the North Africa campaign? What if they resisted Allied landings? The Americans and the British were more than apprehensive, politics were complicated but, in the end, the Army sided with the Allies. True, two-thirds of the FEC in Italy were men from French colonies in North Africa – Algerians, Moroccans, Senegalese, Tunisians, the French Foreign Legion, and they fought splendidly under General Alphonse Juin as part of the US 5th Army. They took and held Belvedere mountains north-east of Cassino, and they opened the road to Rome by their rapid advance through the Aurunchi mountains.

Perhaps it's not surprising that 2,088 FEC men were missing, for what other soldier could have followed in their footsteps across the wild Aurunchi mountains to collect their dead or wounded... only Moroccan mountain troops could have done that, but they only knew how to go forward. The Guams loved to slit German throats, cut German ears off as proof of killing... rape Italian women for war booty, although this was soon put a stop to with a few of their soldiers executed. The entire 15th Army Group in Italy watched with mounting respect how in the fourth and final battle for Monte Cassino and the forcing of the Liri Valley, Moroccan, Algerian, and Tunisian troops achieved what even the Germans thought impossible. General Mark Clark had only words of admiration for the Generals and men of the French Expeditionary Corps. In his own words: "*For this performance, which was to be a key to the success of the entire drive on Rome, I shall always be a grateful admirer of General Juin and his magnificent FEC*"[22]

But turn around, start walking back to town... the same man at the gas station waves even more energetically; perhaps his grandfather or relatives paid for his freedom with their blood, so he appreciates visitors to the cemetery showing respect for their sacrifice. You won't walk very far though before you will stop to look, to absorb and memorize this place –

late October, the sun bathes in a suspension of morning mist, the black soil of newly-ploughed fields contrasts sharply against the fresh green of neighbouring meadows, and a mile or so ahead, Venafro nestles unobtrusively at the foot of Monte Croce and the nearby Monte Sammucro. Oh what a lovely location for a small town – in times of peace, but in times of war? The hills here are strange – huge molehills of rock in a vast meadow, cold, barely covered with a coat of green... docile, even inviting in times of peace, they turned brutal and deadly in the hands of the Germans. And fifty five years later people still remembered; see the writing on that large rock in the town square?

IN REMEBRANCE OF THE TROOPERS
OF THE 504TH PARACHUTE COMBAT TEAM
UNITED STATES ARMY
COLONEL REUBEN H. TUCKER
COMMANDER, COMMAND POST VENAFRO

———————

A TRIBUTE
TO THOSE WHO FOUGHT THEIR LAST
BATTLE WHILE ASSAULTING MOUNT
SAMMUCRO WITH DARING VALOUR
SUFFERING AND MATCHLESS
ACHIEVEMENTS
MAY THEY NEVER BE FORGOTTEN
10 DECEMBER - 27 DECEMBER 1943
DEDICATED DECEMBER 12 1998

What a Christmas they must have had in 1943! The weather was foul. In snow and freezing cold, men from the 504th had to scale near-vertical cliffs to displace well entrenched German positions on Monte Sammucro. Over a period of nineteen days, the 504th suffered 54 dead, 226 wounded, 2 missing.

Cassino - May 1936

A road straight as an arrow leads from the old part of Venafro to the railway station; turn round, take one last look... one more surprise from history. A square keep emerges from the mist in my telephoto lens; it must have been sitting on that cone of scraggy rocks for centuries, inaccessible, invincible until now, for today, a steel bridge spans the void isolating it from the world. And then the final surprise on the way from Venafro to Cassino – my train runs on and on and on through a tunnel black as a moonless night; but at the end of the tunnel, at 20.46 hrs in the evening in Cassino, it is still light, temperature 28°C, people stroll contentedly, enticing aperitifs, pizza, coffee, food and drinks and handicrafts on display, music blares, grownups argue, girls display, boys fight... and the Monastery looks upon it all aloof, cool, inscrutable. But who in this crowd will remember May 1944, the blood, the sacrifice? And what was happening here, in Cassino, at about the same hour on the 9th of May 1936?

For in Rome at about this time on the 9th of May 1936, Piazza Venezia was choking with people in black shirts. A man stepped out onto the balcony of Palazzo Venezia... chin jutting forward, both hands on the balustrade, eyes focused on some point beyond the crowd... immovable, impassive, imperious, oblivious of the populace at his feet - god-like. His arm rises in Roman salute... and the populace falls silent... Friends, Romans and Countrymen! Fascist Italy has now an Empire! I give you Somalia! Fascist Italy now equal France and Great Britain. Italy... a European military power! And the black mass of people goes berserk in adulation. DUCE! DUCE! DUCE! The vision of power, of return to the glory of the old Roman Empire electrifies the Italian nation. And the politicians and the generals at home and in Europe, even Mr. Churchill, begin to look with mounting respect upon this often buffoonish leader of Fascism; even Hitler, that upstart wimp in Mussolini's eyes, came to pay respects and negotiate for support.[23]

Mussolini watched the lectern on the black fascist flag... which way will it point; in which direction will the breeze blow; will fickle military fortunes favour Hitler or the Allies? This great opportunity for the aggrandisement of Fascist Italy must not be missed! In 1939 the flag still hung limply on the balcony of Palazzo Venezia, but in 1940 the political breeze had picked up and the fascist flag pointed decidedly in Hitler's direction. Hitler was moving fast: Poland, Denmark, Norway, Belgium, Holland, France fell like dominos. Fearing he might miss out on the spoils of war, Mussolini acted: on 10 June 1940, Italy declares war on France; 27 September 1940 Italy joins the German-Japan Axis. Italy – now our enemy!

But who knew then how the wheels of fortune would turn, for by the end of 1943 the direction of the storm had changed in favour of the Allies, and fascism had nothing for Italy but misery and destruction. The people of Italy had had enough of fascism and dreams of Roman empire; they wanted to change sides, to be on the winning side… so they shot dead Mussolini and his mistress Clara Petacci, and strung them both up by their feet for all to see that Italian people had a true change of heart. An old woman walked up to the corpse of Clara Petacci and tucked her skirt into her knickers, for like that wasn't proper.[24] Indeed, on 23 October 1943 Italy declared war on its one-time partner – Germany… and became a co-belligerent on the side of the Allies.

10

Epilogue

And seventy years later, October 2013, my walk along the footprints on the Monte Cassino Massive done, I am sitting at its foot in an Italian café, sipping a beer in the warm ambiance of Corso de la Republica, watching the kaleidoscope of colourful, relaxed, happy people leisurely parading in front of me... and reflect on the "bill": 5,600 Italian soldiers killed in the fighting alongside the German armies in North Africa... "only" 945 killed fighting for Italy at the side of the Allies, and now lie in the Italian War Cemetery in Migniano near Cassino?

And France? On so many occasions I sat in Paris sipping a beer in the warm ambiance of Champs Elyse, watching the kaleidoscope of colourful people leisurely parading in front of me, and inevitably reflected on the "bill". From the infamy of defeat of the French army in June 1940, and the pro-German Vichy Government, France was elevated to the level of one of the four powers occupying the defeated Germany - of equal status to the USA, Britain, Soviet Russia! But it was on the back of American and British military might that France was liberated, yet for reasons of "political expediency", the Free French with General de Gaulle at their head were allowed to be first to march into liberated Paris. And was it not for "political expediency" – avoiding even the smallest risk of antagonizing Stalin and the communist regime in Poland - that no one from the earliest and the most loyal Ally at the side of Great Britain - the Polish Armed forces - participated in the Victory Parade in London? And not even after Monte Cassino, not even after the highest British orders of merit were pinned on the chest of Polish Generals?

Perhaps if General Sikorski - the Polish Premier and the Head of the Polish Armed Forces - had not perished in the aeroplane crash off Gibraltar in 1943, the Poles might have found in him a leader able to pursue their vision of an independent Poland as forcefully and consequentially as the lofty General de Gaulle had done for his country.

And I sat in Munich too, in 1958 and '59 and the 60's and 70's in the Hofbrauhause, and watched Germans drink beer by the gallon and consume food by the kilo, and reflected on this shocking "bill"... For with Hitler dead, German armies vanquished, Hitler's elite paratroopers and grenadiers eliminated, German cities bombed out... the German phoenix was already rising on the wind of "political expediency", for Stalin too had a dream of a great Soviet empire and he pursued his ambition relentlessly, ruthlessly, murderously. He outsmarted the Americans, outsmarted the British, annihilated Germans on the Eastern front, and either got what he wanted or took it by force... and the one-time Mr Churchill's and President Roosevelt's great friend-in-need now turned into their enemy No.1. The West was exhausted, weary of war; democracy, and elections at home were on the mind of its leaders... not another bloody war, please! Let Stalin have Poland, Czechoslovakia, the

Baltics, the Balkans… let him keep all he already holds in his grip; the best the West was prepared to do was fight a cold-war… and Germany, our enemy No.1 of only yesterday, became our new greatest friend-in-need of today, growing in strength and power off the billions of dollars from the USA pumped into its economy. And yet, where the Allies drew the line and stood firm, Stalin yielded and retracted his "bill". So I sat in Vienna too, now free of Stalin's tanks and men, drank coffee and ate cake, and to the sound of a waltz thought of Poland… Why? Would the "bill" for its freedom have been too high?

And I sat in Moscow in the 70's and 80's "knocking back vodka" and eating caviar, and when at the conclusion of one particularly successful contract, all bottles were, at long last, empty, the Director of the Investments from the Russian side looks me in the eye, and in a criminal surge of honesty, tells me as it really is: *"Mr Kubica, you come here from America and England to build refineries for us, and when you have built all we need… we will come to your country and build Communism for you"* And I have been "knocking back vodka" in Leningrad too, but on this particular day, *Beriozka*, the foreign currency shop at the hotel was closed to foreigners – only Party Members could shop that day, and as I turned away disappointed, I heard a tour guide explain to a group of tourists: *Poland? Oh that's just another Soviet Republic, well… perhaps not officially.*

So I went to Warsaw, the capital of that *"just another Soviet Republic"*, and sat in a *kawiarnia*, sipped tea and watched the grim kaleidoscope of drab, seemingly empty lives; a shop not quite empty, for one dead chicken dangled from a rail inside, and a long queue of people waiting outside its closed door, waiting patiently for something... for a better future, for liberation from its communist regime, for that "Great" Britain, for America... for that chicken? And what a shocking "bill" – 1,051 lives in Monte Cassino, three times this number in other Polish war cemeteries in Italy, plus the cemeteries in France and the UK, and those buried in the rubble of what once was Warsaw... and more. But the big numbers on the "bill" are already blurred by history – is it a million or two or more dead or abandoned to their fate in Stalin's evil empire? Was this the outcome our Polish fathers had fought for in Libya, Norway, France and Great Britain, and in Belgium, Holland, Italy and Germany... was the price they paid worth their sacrifice *"Za Waszą Wolność i Naszą"*.

And I have been back to Warsaw many times since, in the 80's and 90's, and I was there in May 2013 sitting at a round table in the same *kawiarnia*, being served café-au-lait and French croissants by a young waitress with a smile and surprise at my amazement at what I saw. For that dead chicken has long gone... and that long queue of people gone too! The people got tired of waiting and rose up in *Solidarity* with the miners shot dead by the police at Wójek coalmine, in *Solidarity* with striking dockers in Gdansk, in *Solidarity* with murdered Father Popieluszko, in *Solidarity* against the Moscow-sponsored regime; and they too sat at the *Round Table* negotiating peace, freedom, membership of NATO, membership of the European Union...

The reflections in the shop window amaze me too –

young men with American crew cuts, Poles conversing freely in English, young women smartly dressed, high heels tapping on even pavements, all seemingly in a hurry, all with some objective in mind. And the window itself, now a huge plate of non-reflective smoked glass, above it - the logo of a major foreign bank, behind it – young people with laptops, conversing, working, drinking café lattes. If only I could somehow let my father know that this "*just another Soviet Republic*" is no more, that what he had fought for and his mates bled and died for is right here now... wouldn't he want to come down, go back to Poznań, Wielowieś, perhaps even to Postawy as they are now and, at long last, complete his Odyssey?

It's so easy to settle the bill today – no bombs, no guns, no bayonets needed now…. a small plastic card will do; but as I fish for it in my pocket I find a different kind of bill – an airline ticket back to England, to London to… home! And with it came a feeling of unease, of guilt, for it's not my father - it's me… I have abandoned my father's Odyssey - the Polish Odyssey. And my mind races to find a reason, find an excuse… and all I hear is – well… that's just how it is my boy… that's life man!

Look in the mirror
Who do you see – Man?
What see all others?
The same old – Man?
And at the very end
What were you – Man?
And your Soul now,
Where is it – Man?

Abbreviations,
Sources and Works Cited

3rd DSK – *3 Dywizja Sztrzelców Karpackich* - 3rd Carpathian Riflemen Division
5th KDP – *5 Kresowa Dywizja Piechoty* - 5th Eastern Borderlands Infantry Division

All extracts from Polish sources quoted here have been freely translated by the Author.

1. Adam Majewski, *Wojna Ludzie i Medycyna* Vol. 2, p. 438
2. *Trzecia Dywizja Strzelców Karpackich 1942-1947*, Vol. I. p. 344.
3. Bielatowicz, Jan, *Orzeł Biały* 14. 28 Maj 1944, p 143
4. Feliks Konarski, an extract taken from *Czerwone Maki na Monte Cassino*. The complete lyrics and provenance is given in the Appendix.
5. *Trzecia Dywizja Sztrzelców Karpackich* 1942-1947 Vol.1 p.162
6. Col. Henryk Piątkowski, *Bitwa o Monte Cassino* p. 112
7. Glue W.A and Pringle D.T.C. *20 Battalion and Armoured Regiment*, Ch.15
   http://nzetc.victoria.ac.nz/tm/scholarly/name-001638.html#image-gallery
8. Wańkowicz Melchior, *Bitwa o Monte Cassino* Vol. 3, p. 42
9. ibid. Vol.3, p.273
10. General Wladyslaw Anders, *Bez Ostatniego Rozdziału* 3rd Ed. p. 216
11. Bates P.W. *Supply Company*, Ch. 14, gives a full description of the Inferno Track and this episode at Hove Dump
    http://nzetc.victoria.nz/th/scholarly/tei-WH2Supp--c14.html
12. Adam Majewski, *Wojna Ludzie i Medycyna* p. 411

13. Bielatowicz, Jan, *Orzeł Biały* 14. 28 Maj 1944, p 143

14. Adam Majewski, *Wojna Ludzie i Medycyna* p. 389

15. General Mark Clark, *Calculated Risk*, p. 235

16. Matthew Parker *Monte Cassino* His account provides a well researched description of the events of the Fourth Battle of Monte Cassino p.329

17. ibid p. 339

18. General Mark Clark, *Calculated Risk*, p. 258

19. ibid. p. 267

20. ibid. p. 267

21. www.homeofheroes.com/moh/nisei/index_4cassino.html

22. General Mark Clark, *Calculated Risk*, p. 329

23. Hibbert Christopher *"Benito Mussolini"* p. 1

24. Ibid p.371

Appendix

<u>Czerwone Maki na Monte Cassino</u>
Text by Feliks Konarski (1907 - 1991)
Music by Alfred Schütz (1910 - 1999)

Czy widzisz te gruzy na szczycie?
Tam wróg twój się kryje jak szczur!
Musicie, musicie, musicie!
Za kark wziąć i strącić go z chmur!
I poszli szaleni, zażarci,
I poszli zabijać i mścić,
I poszli jak zawsze uparci,
Jak zawsze za honor się bić.

Refren:
Czerwone maki na Monte Cassino
Zamiast rosy piły polską krew...
Po tych makach szedł żołnierz i ginął,
Lecz od śmierci silniejszy był gniew!
Przejdą lata i wieki przeminą,
Pozostaną ślady dawnych dni!..
I tylko maki na Monte Cassino
Czerwieńsze będą, bo z polskiej wzrosną krwi.

For the full text and English translation see:
http://homepages.ihug.co.nz/~antora/WIERSZE/CASSI
NO/CASSINO.HTM#Red

Bibliography

Anders, Władysław, General, *Bez Ostaniego Rozdziału*, 3rd Edition, 1959 Gryf Publishers Ltd.1959

Bielatowicz, Jan *3 Batalion Strzelców Karpackich*, Atlas Publishers and Distributors, London 1949

Bojakowski, Roman *Pułk 6 Pancerny 'Dzieci Lwowskich' Droga i Przeżycia*, Self published, Londyn 1994

Borucki, Marek *Mussolini*, Książka i Wiedza, 1966

Clark, Mark, General, *Calculated Risk*, George G. Harrap & Co. Ltd. Reprint 1951

Dzikiewicz, Bronisław *Z Teodolitem Pod Monte Cassino*, Wydawnictwo Ministerstw Obrony Narodowej 1984

Gradosielski, Jerzy *5ta KDP Saperzy w Walce 1941-1945*, Self published

Graham, Dominic *Cassino*, The Pan/Ballantine Illustrated History of World War II 1972

Hibbert, Christopher *Benito Mussolini*, Penguin Books, 1965

Kimber William *The Memoirs of Field Marshall Kesselring*

Koło Oddziałowe 17 LBS, *17 Lwowski Batalion Strzelców 'San Angelo'*

Konarski, Feliks *Piosenki z Plecaka Helenki*, Self published, Rome 1944

Kospeth-Pawłoski, Edward et al, *5ta Dywizja Piechoty w Dziejacha Oręża Polskiego*, Biblioteka Historyczna Sztabu Głównego WP, 1947

Maj, Julian *Na Drogach do Piekła*, Wydawnictwo Literackie Kraków, 1973

Majewski, Adam *Wojenne Opowieści Porucznika Szemraja*, Wydawnictwo Lubelskie 1975

Medley, R. H. *Cap Badge* Leo Cooper, 1995

Młotek, Mieczysław (Editor), *Trzecia Dywizja Strzelców Karpackich 1942-1947*, Vol I and II, 1978

New Zealand Electronic Text Collection, *The Official History of New Zealand in the Second World War 1939-1945*, Victoria University of Wellington

Parker, Matthew *Monte Cassino*, Headline Book Publishing, 2004

Piątkowski, Henryk *Bitwa o Monte Cassino*, Oddział Kultury i Prasy 2go Korpusu, 1946

Ramię Pancerne 2 Polskiego Korpusu, Wydawnictwo Referenta Kultury i Pracy 2 Warszawskiej Dywizji Pancernej, Rome 1946

Wańkowicz, Melchior *Bitwa o Monte Cassino*, Wydawnictwo Oddziału. Kultury i Prasy 2go Polskiego Korpusu, Rzym, 1945

William Kimber & Company Ltd. *The Memoirs of Field Marshal Kesselring*

Maps, Trails and GPS Coordinates

A useful map of trails on the Monte Cassino Massive is
provided at: http://montecairotrekking.it

Source: Glue W.A, Pringle D.J.C *20 Battalion and Armoured Regiment*

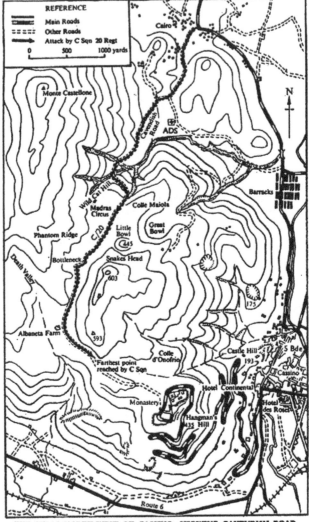

THE HILLS NORTH-WEST OF CASSINO, SHOWING CAVENDISH ROAD AND ROUTE OF TANK ATTACK

Cavendish Road / Droga Polskich Saperow

The Inferno Track / Droga do Piekła

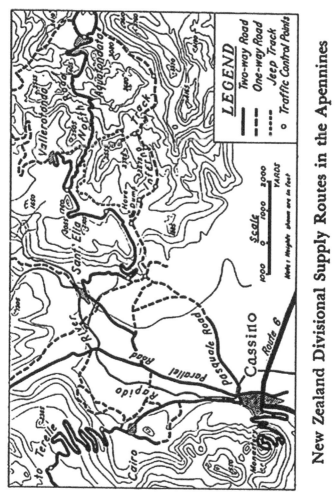

Source: Bates P.W. *Supply Company*

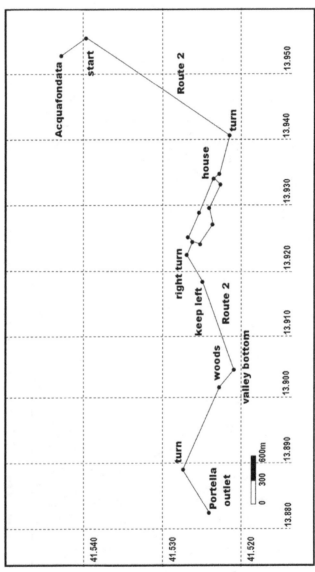

Inferno Track Trail (GPS coordinates page 161)

Big-Small Bowl Trail (GPS coordinates page 161)

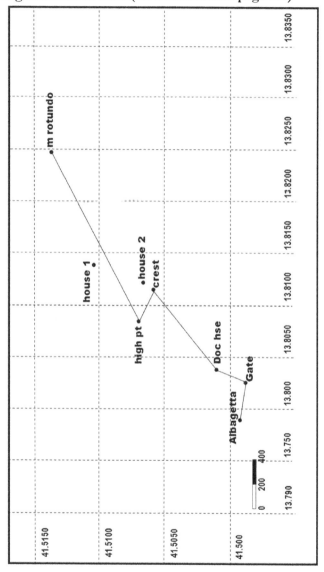

GPS Coordinates for the Inferno Track

Acquafondata	N41.5426 E13.9532	Alt 913m.
Start	N41.5395 E13.9559	Alt 880m.
Enter Inferno	N41.1997 E13.9560	Alt 870m.
Big bend	N41.5208 E13.9405	Alt 950m.
House	N41.5260 E13.9214	Alt 760m.
Rock fall	N41.5230 E13.9129	Alt 690m.
Pit	N41.5216 E13.9086	Alt 613m.
Track forks	N41.5225 E13.9008	Alt 477m.
Last bend	N41.5275 E13.8892	Alt 317m.
Out Portella	N41.5234 E13.8734	Alt 190m.

GPS Coordinates for the Big & Small Bowl Trail

M. Rotondo	N41.5150 E13.8285	Alt 67m.
Start Big B	N41.5141 E13.8234	Alt 93
Pin head	N41.5139 E13.8155	Alt 252
Gate	N41.5103 E13.8156	Alt 347
Left fork	N41.5088 E13.8126	Alt 380
Crest B/S	N415062 E13.8083	Alt 477
Right turn	N41.5056 E13.8092	At 490
Summit	N41.5049 E13.8054	Alt 530

Points of interest - GPS coordinates

Monastery	N41.4896 E13.8131	Alt 490m.
Albanetta	N41.4978 E13.7980	Alt 465
Tank	N41.5007 E 13.7995	Alt. 505
Point-593	N41.4971 E13.8023	Alt 564
Doc's House	N41.5015 E13.8040	Alt 575
Point-575	N41.4993 E13.7904	Alt 540
St Angelo	N41.5073 E13.7910	Alt 580
Essex Mon.	N41.4948 E13.8246	Alt 155
Beds-Hamps	N41.4700 E13.8353	Alt 35
Bell of Peace	N41.4436 E13.8349	Alt 27
Piedimonte	N41.5039 E13.7511	Alt 220
Venafro	N41.4855 E14.0464	Alt 668

Photographic images

The original photographs of the images sourced from publications in the New Zealand Electronic Text Collection (**NZETC**) are reproduced with permission of The New Zealand Ministry for Culture and Heritage.

All other photographs, with the exception of the "Big Bowl", are reproduced with permission of Alexander Turnbull Library, National Library of New Zealand.

Photographs from Monte Cassino in 2012-13 were taken by the Author.

Source of photo. NZETC, Phillips, N.C. *Italy Vol.1,* 1957
(Photographer A.M. Miller)

The first stick of bombs falls on Cassino, 15 March 1944

The Monastery, shortly after the bombing. February
1944. Source: Alexander Turnbull Library, New Zealand
PAColl-4161-08 Ref.DA-03751-F (L.H. Ross)

Cassino's "day of doom" - 15/03/1944. Source:

NZETC, Phillips N.C. *Italy Vol.1, 1957*

Cassino after the battle. Source: NZETC, Phillips, N.C. *Italy Vol.1,* 1957 (G.R. Bull)

After bombing – May 1944. Source: Alexander Turnbull Library, New Zealand (PAColl-4161-08) Ref. DA-05693- F (G.F. Kaye)

Albanetta, February 1944. Source: NZETC, Glue W.A., Pringle D.J.C. *20 Battalion and Armoured Regiment*

Big Bowl, May 1944. Source: Romuald Lipinski, via
Kresy-Siberia Virtual Museum.

American, French and Indian mule teams. Feb 1944.
Source Alexander Turnbull Library, New Zealand PAColl-
4161-08

Source: NZETC, McKinney J.B. *Medical Units of 2 NZEF in Middle East and Italy,* 1952 (K.G. Killoh)

5 ADS, Cassino, March 1944

A FIELD OPERATING THEATRE
—a surgical team applies a Thomas splint, *Cassino*

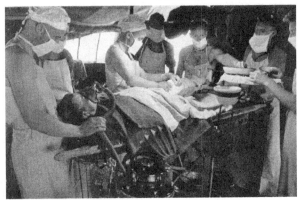

Source: NZETC, McKinney J.B. *Wounded in Battle, Episodes & Studies, Vol.1*

Source: NZETC, Robin Kay, *Italy Vol. II*, 1967, (G.F. Kaye)

Evacuating civilians from the battlefront

THE ITALIANS CHANGED THEIR MINDS and followed
cheerfully towards Eighth Army's lines (page 10)

Source: NZETC, Robin Kay, *Italy Vol. II*, 1967, (G.F.Kaye)

Polish War Cemetery - fragment

Monument to 4 Pulk Broni Pancernej

Monument to 5 Kresowa Dywizja Piechoty

Monument to 3 Brygada Strzelców Karpackich

Piedimonte – Polish Memorial

The Essex Regiment - Monument

Bedfordshire and Hertfordshire Monument

Sant' Angelo – Ho Bell of Peace

Made in the USA
Monee, IL
27 November 2021

83182420R00111